GERMAN PROSE
COMPOSITION
FOR SIXTH FORMS

GERMAN PROSE COMPOSITION FOR SIXTH FORMS

BY

W. M. DUTTON M.A.

SOMETIME ASSISTANT MODERN LANGUAGE MASTER
MERCHANT TAYLORS' SCHOOL

HARRAP   LONDON

First published in Great Britain 1954
by GEORGE G. HARRAP & CO. LTD
182 High Holborn, London WC1V 7AX

Reprinted: 1956: 1958; 1961; 1962; 1964;
1966; 1969; 1971; 1973; 1975; 1976; 1977;
1979

ISBN 0 245 50696 9

Printed in Great Britain by
Biddles Ltd, Guildford, Surrey

PREFACE

THIS book provides proses for use as a two-year course leading from "O" to "A" level. Six proses set in recent years in the Oxford and Cambridge Schools Examination Board Higher Certificate and "A and S" level examination are printed at the end by kind permission of the Board. In order that they may be used as test pieces no vocabulary or notes are given.

The acquisition of an adequate vocabulary, with a consequent increase in fluency, is the big step to be made at this stage, and while nothing can replace wide reading for this purpose, it is almost impossible to harness prose work directly to current reading matter. The subjects of these proses have therefore been made as varied as possible, and the vocabulary can, of course, be systematically enlarged by the addition by the teacher of cognate words, synonyms, etc., to the ones actually required for the translation.

It is often found that better results are obtained if each prose is worked through and the necessary vocabulary provided in class before a written version is attempted, and it is in order to facilitate this method that the vocabulary is very full and has been arranged in blocks corresponding to each prose but placed at the end of the book. Once the vocabulary has been thoroughly mastered and any grammatical points dealt with, the prose can be written as an unseen, apart from the suggestions in the notes with each prose. It is usually found more profitable to suggest the correct word in advance than to attempt the eradication of misconceptions arrived at from the excessive use of the dictionary.

If translations are required, a set   is available, for teachers only, on application to the publishers.

My thanks are due to Mrs T. E. Griffits and to Studienreferendar F. W. Weisshaupt for reading the manuscript and offering many valuable suggestions.

W. M. D.

CONTENTS

FIRST YEAR

1. VILLAGE HOLIDAY

Every year my brothers and sisters and I used to spend a month in [1] the country with our mother. We lived in a village not more than 50 miles from London, but my father could not make the journey every day. He came for [2] two days each week-end and usually spent one whole week with us at the end of the month. The house was not large and the rent must have been moderate for we were not rich. I often heard my mother saying [3] to her friends in town that it was worth it because the month gave us health enough for the whole year. Some people would find it boring always to spend the summer holidays in the same place, but we were always very happy. There were so many things that were different from at home. In our life there one particular circumstance always delighted us. Nothing came to us at second hand. If we wanted milk or eggs [4] we went to the farm; vegetables came straight from [5] the garden and not from a shop, and even water [6] we drew from the well in [7] a bucket.

1. *auf.* 2. *auf* with Acc. 3. Tr. "say." 4. Insert *so*.
5. *direkt aus.* 6. Add Def. Art. 7. Tr. "with."

2. A CONVERSATION

"How long have you been in London, Miss Emsing?"
"Nearly a fortnight." [1]
"And how do you like it [2] here?"
"Oh, very well thank you."

"You have seen [3] many of the sights already, I suppose?" [4]

"Unfortunately not. I have had very few opportunities [5] up to now. You see, I am not here on holiday. I have a post in a hospital as a [6] nurse."

"You speak English extraordinarily well."

"I don't understand everything yet. But I came chiefly in order to improve my English. Naturally I learned English at [7] school."

"We learn languages, too, but we never speak them as well as foreigners speak English. We must be less enterprising."

"Or less cheeky and talkative!"

"What has made the greatest impression on you here?"

"The traffic, I think. I come from [8] a small town and it is quite new to me. The Underground is the latest invention for me."

"I hope [9] you are not homesick?"

"No. Not yet anyway. The other nurses [10] are very kind and have taken a lot of trouble over me."

"I am glad of that.[11] Now I must find our hostess and take my leave. I want to avoid the crush on the way home. Good-bye, Miss Emsing, I am glad [11] to have met you."

1. No exact equivalent. Tr. "two weeks" or "fourteen days." 2. Use *gefallen* (with Dat.). 3. *besichtigen.* 4. Tr. *wohl.* 5. Use sing. 6. Omit "a." 7. *in der.* 8. *stammen aus.* 9. *hoffentlich.* 10. A German girl would say *meine Kolleginnen.* 11. Use *sich freuen.*

3. THE OLD FARMER

The old farmer sat in a comfortable armchair on the lawn, a sheep dog at his feet. His two grandchildren came out of the house and stopped for a moment beside his chair. They carried fishing rods on their shoulders.[1]

"Where are you going?" [2] asked the old man.

"Down to the river," the two boys replied. "We want to catch a few trout."

"Be careful they don't catch you and pull you in." The boys smiled politely, for they liked their grandfather who was very generous. Here in the holidays they were allowed to go anywhere and do anything.

"Don't go to the mill in any case," he went on. "The water is too deep there and it is dangerous."

"Don't worry, grandfather. We shall be careful."

And the boys set off. Before they had gone out of the garden the dog barked, looked at his master and wagged his tail. "All right. Off you go," [3] he said, and the dog followed the boys. He went over the fence as they had done,[4] all three considering the gate quite superfluous.

The old man had the morning paper in his hand, but he did not unfold it. He just [5] sat in the bright sunshine and watched the children and the dog as they went down the road in the direction of the river. They disappeared and the farmer closed his eyes and slept.

1. Sing. 2. Remember he is speaking to two children. 3. *also, los.* 4. Add "it." 5. *einfach.*

4. AT THE ZOO

When the children reached the lions and tigers they were almost afraid, for the animals were roaring impatiently. Feeding time for the carnivores was at two o'clock and they only had to wait ten minutes till the men brought the huge pieces of meat. These were thrust through the bars into the cages [1] and were at once seized, torn to pieces and devoured. Then the big creatures yawned, stretched themselves, and dozed with half shut eyes. "Just like our cat," said John. "Except that their paws are nearly as big as your head," replied Mary, "and just [2] look at their claws." "I want to feed the monkeys with the monkey nuts I have brought," said George. They gave away the nuts and then they visited the sea lions and seals who were diving and swimming about [3] in their pool. The elephant skilfully took cake from their hands with his long trunk and all [4] their supply of food was gone.[5] They had seen so much they were getting tired, and it was already four o'clock. They went slowly to the exit and went home by bus. The next time they specially wanted to see the hippopotamus and the ostrich, but they had seen enough for one day.

1. Add *hinein*. 2. *mal*. 3. *umher*. 4. *ganz*. 5. *alle* (invar.).

5. THE BAY

"Not a [1] step farther," said Aunt Christine and sat down on the sand. It was a lovely spot at the foot of the cliffs. From top to bottom was at least 300 feet, [2] a steep and rugged slope, and the seagulls circled and glided to and fro over their heads.

The smaller children collected seaweed and brightly coloured stones until they discovered a cave. Then they played pirates and poor [3] Aunt Christine was captured. The others undressed and swam in the surf until they were [4] tired. Then they lay on the rocks and read or slept in the warm sun. After tea Aunt Christine suggested that they should swim once more before they went back to the hotel. The little ones had naturally collected so much that they could not possibly [5] carry everything and they had to leave the seaweed and most of their crabs and stones behind. Eric and Henry wanted to climb up the cliff, but they were not allowed [6] to try. "We shall have to [7] if we don't hurry," remarked Laura. "Look at the water. The tide will soon reach the corner of the bay. Or perhaps the lifeboat would rescue us. How marvellous!" But Aunt Christine thought otherwise and they walked home.

1. Acc. 2. Use Sing. Can be given in metres. 3. Def. Art. required before Proper Noun preceded by Adj. 4. *waren* or *wurden*? 5. Tr. *unmöglich konnten.* 6. Remember *erlauben* takes the Dat. and therefore cannot be used in the Passive except impersonally. 7. Add "do it."

6. THE HILL

They reached the summit of the hill together and threw themselves breathless and panting on the dry grass. It was wonderfully refreshing up there after the strenuous climb; a breeze that was as good as a cool drink stirred their hair and blew out their matches when they lit their cigarettes. Far below them the plain was spread out like a map where the river wound its way like a shining ribbon. The meadows were divided by [1] hedges in whose shadow the cattle sought refuge from [2] the heat of the sun. The cornfields had every shade of yellow and gold, but it was impossible from so great a distance to identify the wheat, the barley, and the oats. The hay harvest was long since over and new haystacks stood in the corner of many meadows. Those patches of brown would be [3] ploughland and the stretches of [4] darker green were presumably root crops or cabbages. [5] There was no activity to be seen down there. The only moving object was a train which came slowly, like a toy, into sight trailing [6] a cloud of smoke. Up here a hawk hovered, the larks sang invisible and rabbits hopped about on the grass in front of the hawthorn bushes.

1. *durch.*   2. *vor.*   3. *waren wohl.*   4. Tr. "of a."   5. Sing.
6. Tr. "and trailed."

7. WEINSBERG

At the beginning of the twelfth century the castle of[1] Weinsberg, not far from Stuttgart, was besieged. The outcome of this siege is often quoted as an example of feminine courage and faithfulness. Many brave men on both sides had fallen in the bitter fighting, [2] but the garrison's worst enemy was [3] hunger. King Conrad, who led the army which had surrounded the stronghold, swore he would show mercy to no man even if the gates were opened. The women [4] of Weinsberg asserted their innocence and he said they might [5] depart unharmed. They might [5] take with them their dearest possessions, as much as they could carry on their backs. On the following morning the great gates opened and a strange procession tottered slowly out. Each woman was carrying her husband on her shoulders. Many of the enemy soldiers said they had been tricked and wanted to strike them all down, but the King would [6] not permit it. "No," he said, "I will keep my word." And so the men of Weinsberg were saved by their faithful wives.

1. Omit "of." 2. *Kämpfen.* 3. Def. Art. needed. 4. In the famous legend they are called *Weiber*, but this is seldom used nowadays for "women." 5. Use *dürfen.* 6. NOT *würde.*

8. ON THE CHURCH TOWER

The view was wonderful and the boys had taken a map with them so that they could name the woods, hills, and villages to be seen [1] in the distance. They had spent more than an hour up there when it occurred to them that they ought to go home. They went down the spiral staircase, but when they reached the door which led into the church they found that it was locked. "What do we do now?" said Peter after they had beaten on the door for a time and shouted as loud as they could. "They would hear us better, perhaps, if we were at the top of the tower," suggested Walter. But the tower was high and tall trees divided the churchyard from the village street. "It will soon be dark," said Peter. "We must try something else." He considered for a moment. "Yes, the bells," he said. "Come [2] on." He led Walter to the place where the bells hung, but it was impossible to ring them. Then Walter caught sight of a broom leaning against the wall. At [3] the third attempt he succeeded [4] in catching [5] one of the bells a hefty blow with the handle. The noise was deafening and not until [6] it had died away could the boys hear themselves speak. "People must be pretty deaf if they don't hear that," said Walter. And indeed it was [7] not long before the Vicar and a few other men came to the church to see what was going on.

1. Tr. "which were to be seen" (*zu sehen*). 2. Omit "on." 3. *Bei.* 4. *gelang es ihm.* 5. Infin. 6. *erst als.* 7. *dauerte es.*

9. ARRIVAL

First [1] left, second right. That is, if he had understood [2] what the policeman was saying. He had learned how to ask [3] questions of that kind, but that had been in his own classroom where the teacher could correct him when he made a mistake. It was quite a different matter [4] to address a real German in [5] the street, and the reply had been spoken so quickly and with an unexpected accent. It would probably get easier when he had grown accustomed to it, but thank goodness Hans knew [6] English. All the same he would have been glad if someone had met [7] him at the station, though he could hardly have expected [8] it, since he had arrived by [9] an earlier train than had been arranged. He hoped Hans' [10] family would be as decent as Hans himself and that they would not laugh at him if he forgot the verb in the middle of a long sentence. That boy on a bicycle on the wrong side of the road looked very like Hans. Yes, it was Hans. "Hello, Hans," he called out in English. Hans rode over to him, held out his hand, and greeted him in German. "I am sorry," began John. "I don't understand any [11] English now, John," answered Hans. "When I was in England I had to speak English, now it is your turn." [12] "I will try," [13] said John, "but you speak English so well." "Only because you taught me," said Hans. "Come, give me your suitcase. It is not much further to our flat. It is grand to see you again. How is your family?"

1. Add "street." 2. Insert *das*. 3. Use *man*. 4. Tr. "something quite different." 5. Prep? 6. Verb? 7. Tr. "fetched." 8. Watch verb order. 9. *mit*. 10. Apostrophe needed, but only after names ending with a sibilant. 11. Tr. "understand no English." 12. Now it is my turn, "*jetzt bin ich daran*." 13. Insert *es*.

10. THE PRISONER OF WAR

He had come through the wood without difficulty and was about to [1] run towards the quarry when a bullet hit him in the leg. He fell to the [2] ground and had not even time to draw his pistol before two enemy soldiers seized his arms. He closed his eyes and waited for [3] death, for the battle had been long and fierce. But they did not kill him. They disarmed him, lifted him up, and since he could not walk they carried him, one after the other on their shoulders. He guessed that they were carrying him to their headquarters [4] and tried to memorize the direction, but the pain was too severe and he lost consciousness. When he came to himself again he lay on the floor of a bare room. There was no bed, but his wound had been bound up and a rough blanket drawn over him. Beside him stood a glass of water. Presently the door opened and a soldier came into the room. He brought bread and soup and the news that he would soon have a visit, [5] from an old acquaintance. When the latter entered after a quarter of an hour he had to stoop in the doorway [6] because he was so tall. "Well, Captain," [7] he said. "We were expecting you."

1. *wollte eben.* 2. Omit "the." 3. Def. Art. needed. 4. Sing. 5. *Besuch bekommen.* 6. Tr. "door." 7. Any title, military or civilian, is preceded by *Herr*.

11. THE COUSIN FROM CANADA

The distance from the village was greater than I had imagined, and when I stood at length in front of the house I was tired and thirsty. The countryside was very pretty, but the house itself was ugly. It resembled a box made from dirty yellow bricks, and the garden in front [1] where a few wretched hens scratched among nettles and weeds [2] looked neglected. I had the feeling that unseen eyes had been furtively watching my arrival although no movement was to be seen. Smoke rose from one of the chimneys and behind the house washing hung on a line. I had not yet seen my cousin but I had the impression that my stay here would be as short as possible. But it was stupid to think of [3] going away [4] before I had even arrived, so I went to the door and knocked; there was no bell. I waited. Then I knocked again. After a long pause I heard steps in [5] the hall. A key turned groaning in the lock and two bolts were drawn back. Then the door was opened a little and an old woman looked at me suspiciously through the crack. "Is the [6] Doctor at home, please?" I inquired. Then I added, "I have come from [7] Canada to see him." That was not really quite true, but the old woman looked at me from head to foot as though I had come straight from gaol. "Just a minute," [8] she said and shut the door again.

1. *vorne.* 2. Sing. 3. *an.* 4. *das Weggehen.* 5. *auf.* 6. Add *Herr.* 7. *aus.* 8. *Augenblick mal.*

12. SHIPWRECK

"Let's [1] play shipwreck," suggested Toni. One [2] wet afternoon the children were in the schoolroom. The little girl was playing with her [3] dolls, but the boys sat by the window and were bored, for there was nothing to see but [4] rain. "All right," [5] said his brother. "We are the only survivors and we are on an island in the middle of the Pacific." "Yes, and we both had just time [6] to collect three things before the ship was wrecked. What have you brought?" "An axe, a saw and a gun." "And I have a box of matches," said Toni. "No, a magnifying glass, I mean. The sun shines here every day and we can light a fire with it when we need it to cook our food. A knife and a note-book so that we can describe our adventures. We were nearly drowned when we were struggling with the waves and we must have a rest.

Here are some dry leaves. We can lie down on them."
He took some cushions and they made a bed. After a
few minutes Toni groaned. "It's no use," he said;
"I'm hungry and I can't sleep." "Look, here's a piece
of chocolate," said his brother. "That doesn't count as
one of my three things—I had it in my pocket." It was
a real piece of chocolate and still edible, although rather
dirty. "Now we must build a house in a tree before
nightfall in case there are savages or snakes." "There
never are any [7] in the stories," objected Toni. "Only
monkeys and goats and they are always useful, at least
the goats are. Oh yes, I remember, the monkeys throw
coconuts at [8] us, and that saves us when we are dying
of [9] thirst and haven't found the spring of [10] fresh water
yet. We make a hole in the shell with the knife and drink
the liquid." "I am going to eat turtle eggs for breakfast. We shall find them in the sand. Hard boiled?"

1. The imperative as a suggestion is often *wir wollen.* . . .
2. Add "on." 3. There is no need to make possessive adj.
agree with words like *das Mädchen, das Fräulein.* 4. *als.* 5.
schön. 6. *gerade Zeit genug.* 7. *welche.* 8. *nach.* 9. *vor.* 10. *mit.*

13. THE ENVY OF THE GODS

The Tyrant of Samos stood on the roof of his palace
and looked down on the island he ruled. To his friend
Amasis, King of Egypt, who stood by his side, he said,
"All this is mine. Am I not fortunate?" "Fortune is
kind to you indeed. Those who were once [1] your equals
are now your subjects. Yet one still lives. . . ." But
the arrival of a messenger interrupted him. The
messenger bore, as a gift sent by General Polydore, the
head of just [2] that very rival. "Two dangers still
threaten," said the King. "Your fleet may be wrecked

in the storm, and the Cretan army is approaching these shores." [3] Hardly were the words spoken when the fleet, laden with booty, came to anchor in the harbour and the sailors reported with jubilation that the enemy's army had been destroyed in the storm. "Beware the envy of the Gods," said the King. "You must try to propitiate them by the sacrifice [4] of your dearest possession." The Tyrant took a ring and threw it into the sea. But on the following day there came a fisherman before his lord and presented him with a great fish he had caught. "The finest I have ever caught, my Lord," he said. When the cook cut up the fish he found the costly ring in its stomach. He hastened to the Tyrant. "Your luck knows no bounds, my Lord," he cried. "Look, here is the ring you threw into the sea." The King of Egypt waited not a moment longer, but took ship in order not to be there when the Gods dashed his friend to pieces.

1. *einst.*   2. *gerade.*   3. Sing.   4. *das Opfer* is the object sacrificed. Use the verbal noun.

14. BELSHAZZAR

It was just before midnight and the ancient city of Babylon lay still, sunk in [1] sleep. Only up in the King's palace the King feasted with his retinue in wild abandon. In the light of flickering torches, wine and words flowed free and the King's face glowed with [2] wine and pride. Unnoticed, he gave a secret order to a servant. The servant disappeared from the banquet hall and when he returned he bore on his head many gold and silver vessels which had been stolen from Jehovah's temple. Belshazzar seized a goblet, filled it with wine [3] to the brim and emptied it at [4] a draught. Then with wild blasphemies he hurled scorn and defiance at God. Finally with crazy arrogance he shouted, "My name is Belshazzar, King of Babylon." The laughter fell silent. With trembling limbs everyone sat full of fear and dread. Then slowly a monstrous hand appeared, traced letters of fire on the whitewashed wall, wrote and disappeared. Pale as death, the King sent for his magi. "Interpret [5] me this writing and I will clothe you in purple and hang a golden chain about your necks," he said. But the magi stood dumb. Then Daniel was sent for. "Keep your [6] gifts," he said, "Yet will I interpret the writing. Mene; that is, God hath numbered thy kingdom and finished it. Tekel; that is, thou art weighed in the balances and art found wanting. [7] Peres; that is, thy kingdom is divided and given to the Medes [8] and the Persians." [9] And in that very [10] night the King was slain.

1. *im.* 2. *vor.* 3. Insert *bis.* 4. *in* with Dat, or *auf* with Acc. 5. Use the *du* form in the plural. 6. *deine.* 7. Tr. "found too light." 8. *Meder.* 9. *Perser.* 10. Tr. "same."

15. MRS BRANDT GOES SHOPPING

Mrs Brandt put on her hat. She had to go into town to do some shopping. Not in itself a difficult undertaking, but not for [1] fifteen years had she felt like this. [2] Then [3] she had been a little girl and her mother had sent her—for the first time quite alone—to the baker's to buy bread. They had smiled at her in the shop and had called her "Miss." That had been literally child's play, now it was serious. [4] As [5] a housewife she was responsible for the housekeeping and if she made a mistake! She shook herself free of these childish thoughts, made sure that she had enough money in her purse, that the door key was in her handbag, picked up [6] her basket and went to the bus stop. She got out at the post office. Stamps, that was easy and, besides, the clerk at the counter was an old acquaintance. Then with beating heart she went to the butcher's. Beef, mutton, pork, veal—how did one [7] distinguish? And how much did a husband eat? And how expensive everything was. But the butcher was very polite and so were the trades-people in the other shops. "Yes, Mrs Brandt, No, Mrs Brandt, certainly not. Anything else today?" [8] After a difficult victory no Army commander could have been happier or more tired than Mrs Brandt in the bus on the way home.

1. *seit.* 2. Tr. "had this feeling." 3. *damals.* 4. . . . *war es Ernst.* 5. Remember that *als* is "in the capacity of," *wie* is "like"; the article is omitted with *als*, included with *wie*. 6. Tr. "took." 7. Use *sollen.* 8. *sonst etwas gefällig?*

16. AUTUMN IN THE MOUNTAINS

The cows walked slowly across the wooden bridge. On [1] a leather strap round each neck dangled a bell which tinkled or rang with a high or low note, according to [2] its size. This soft music was as gentle as the animals themselves, which were small, dainty creatures with enormous eyes. Behind them strolled a small boy wearing leather trousers and white stockings. In his hand he held a switch with which he cut the heads off the thistles growing at the wayside. [3] As he went across the bridge he threw the switch into the water and stood there for a moment to watch it as the stream carried it swiftly away. He did not need it any more. In winter the cows always stayed down [4] in the village and not till [5] the spring of the following year would he drive them again to the meadows up [6] on the mountain. As soon as the sun sank behind the high peaks it already grew very cold in the valley. Up there the summits were bathed in fiery red by the last rays. At [7] that great height the snow could never melt, but in many places the precipices were so steep that no snow could lie. Between the largest peaks the bottom [8] edge of the glacier, whose melting ice fed [9] the stream the cows had just crossed, came down almost as far as the highest trees. The last mountaineers had gone and the winter sports enthusiasts were not [5] to be expected for six weeks. The boy shut the cows in and then went indoors himself.

1. *an.* 2. *je nach,* 3. *am Wege.* 4. *unten.* 5. Use *erst.* 6. *oben.* 7. *in.* 8. *untere.* 9. Tr. "filled."

17. MISS SCRATTON

Since the death of her father in the autumn of the previous year Miss Scratton had had very little to do, for she was now quite alone. The other members of the family did not purposely neglect her, but they were all busy with their own affairs. At [1] the funeral her married sisters had said, "Oh, you must pay us a long visit now that [2] you are free," but she knew that it was only out of kindness and that she would be in their way. Yes, now she was indeed free, but she had spent so many years without freedom that she was only just [3] beginning to perceive the meaning of the word. She could in fact do what she liked. She had inherited quite a considerable sum of money—her reward for all those wasted years. "No, not wasted," she added hastily, although it had been no easy task. And then the letter had come from South Africa, from a dear friend who had long ago married and had emigrated with her husband.

It [4] contained a warm invitation to spend a year on their estate. Without hesitation she accepted the invitation and went at once to the travel bureau to inquire about the journey.

1. *bei.* 2. *da.* 3. *erst jetzt.* 4. Gender?

18. MARTIN LUTHER

Everyone knows that Martin Luther is supposed to have flung his inkwell at [1] the devil. It must be true, for you can still see the mark on [2] the wall. But that alone would not explain why he is so important in [3] history. What else did he do?

Martin Luther was born in the year 1483 at [4] Eisleben in Saxony. At the age of 18 he went to [5] the University of Erfurt. His father, a man of humble origin, would have been content if his son had become a [6] lawyer, but he entered a monastery and became a monk. His great struggle with [7] the Pope and the Catholic Church began in 1517 a few years after a journey to Rome which [8] filled him with horror. The Church called his writings and opinions heretical, but many people listened to him, for his sermons made a great impression. Those who followed him were called Protestants. In 1521 Luther was in danger of his life and he lived for a time hidden in a castle called the Wartburg. While he was here he wrote his wonderful translation of the Bible into German.

He had a strange, passionate mind, but there is no doubt that he was one of the most influential men of his time.

1. Prep.? 2. *auf* or *an?* 3. *in der.* 4. *zu.* 5. *auf.* with Acc.; omit "of." 6. Omit "a." 7. *mit* or *gegen.* 8. All names of towns are Neuter.

19. IN AN ART GALLERY

Jan was bored to death. He knew nothing about art, and he had been in the art gallery for three-quarters of an hour. He had only come in because he had refused to bring his mackintosh with him.[1] When it had suddenly begun to rain he had taken refuge here without thinking. Right [2] at the entrance he had a disagreeable surprise when he had to pay 1s. 6d. admission fee, but it was too late then. He yawned and went to the window for the third time in ten minutes. The rain was still streaming down the window panes but the sky looked a little brighter. Soon perhaps he would be able to escape. Feeling more cheerful he returned to the pictures. In this room there were mostly drawings and engravings with a few water-colours here and there. He wandered back to the oil paintings which at least had bright colours. Suddenly he noticed a picture he had not seen before. He looked at it with careful interest, for sailing [3] was his speciality. Then a grin spread [4] over his youthful countenance. "Do you like it?" inquired a voice behind him. "The only picture in the gallery that has interested me," he replied. "At least it is funny." "Funny? Why?" "Well,[5] you see, I like the water and the sky. They look just like that on a windy day; but the boat! If it really had had the sails set like that [6] in [7] such a strong wind it must have sunk before the picture was finished." "Thank you very much," said the man. "If only someone had told me that sooner. You see, I painted the picture myself."

1. Omit "him." 2. *schon.* 3. Verbal noun. 4. Use *gehen.* 5. *Na.* 6. *so.* 7. *bei.*

20. THE WEATHER

As he came out of the hotel dining-room [1] Mr Theobald tapped the barometer. He sat down in his usual place and addressed the periodical in the armchair beside him. "I believe it will be fine [2] again tomorrow." The periodical was lowered, disclosing the amiable features of the Bishop, clearly willing to pursue any [3] topic of conversation, though it be only the weather. "Yes, to be sure," [4] he replied, "though probably no farmer would agree with us after this long drought. It would be impossible, would it not?" [5] he continued "to satisfy all the varied wishes that are expressed with regard to the weather. Townsfolk such as [6] you and I hardly take the weather into account. It forms the background to our normal life, that is all.[7] We grumble at the rain and cold and are cheered by a fine day, but it has no great influence on [8] what we do or when we carry it out. For many people, however, for farmers, sailors, aeroplane pilots, professional sportsmen, the weather is a very serious matter." "I think," interrupted Mr Theobald, "that you exaggerate the indifference of the town dweller to the weather in one respect. So many of us are on holiday at this time of the year, that whatever [9] our occupation at home may be, we are agreed on one thing,[10] in wishing [11] for fine weather tomorrow."

1. Tr. "dining-room of the hotel." 2. Tr. "we shall have fine weather." 3. *ein jedes.* 4. *gewiss.* 5. *nicht wahr?* 6. *wie.* 7. *sonst nichts.* 8. Tr. "neither on what we do nor on the time when. . . ." 9. *was . . . auch.* 10. *darüber.* 11. Tr. "when we wish."

21. THE OLD FLOWER-SELLER

Every day, in winter as in summer, the old woman with her baskets of flowers [1] was always on the same spot. She sat on the steps of the fountain opposite the museum and my father told me he could not remember a time when she had not been there. With her black hat and black dress, her big, coloured umbrella, she belonged to the square like the fountain itself. She was very fat and was as cheerful as fat people are as a rule. People bought her flowers not only because they were cheap and always fresh, but because of [2] her happy smile too. For the business men going to [3] their offices in the morning the day had hardly begun properly until they had said "good morning" to old Lise and bought a carnation or a bunch of heather from her for their buttonhole. The young policemen treated her with respect for she had a sharp tongue and was old enough besides to be their grandmother. The older policemen nodded to her as they walked by and said, "How are you today?" Her reply was always the same, "Haven't you arrested anyone yet?" Sometimes a young man and a girl stopped in front of her. The young man would buy a rose or a bunch of violets for the girl and while she fastened the flowers with a pin Lise would say, "Going to the theatre, my dear? You look very pretty today. Have a good time!" [4] An artist had even painted a portrait of her and although he was famous and she was only a poor old woman, she refused to go to his studio. No, he had to paint her [5] where she was at home, on the steps of the fountain.

1. One word. 2. *wegen.* 3. *in.* 4. *Viel Vergnügen.* 5. Insert *dort.*

22. AN INTERRUPTED MEAL

"Do you like [1] beans or do you prefer cauliflower? Please help yourself. They are both out of our garden," said Mrs Smallways. "Thank you," answered Mrs Longford. "I envy you. Vegetables [2] taste so much better when they are really fresh. I often regret that we have no garden and that we cannot grow our own vegetables." [2] "I often wonder whether it is worth while," said Mr Smallways. "This year, for example, the birds ate [3] almost all the strawberries and the peas before we could pick them. And then the weather; it can't possibly [4] be favourable for everything. If it is too hot and dry in summer, we shall have no brussels sprouts [5] next winter and if it rains too often [6] the tomatoes will not ripen. I am thankful that I am not a farmer." Mrs Smallways was just [7] handing her friend a bowl of raspberries when the conversation was interrupted by the ringing of the telephone. "Excuse me," said Mr Smallways. In a moment he returned. "I am sorry, but I must go to the mine at once. There has been [8] an accident. Not very serious, I hope,[9] but a man has been hurt. I will be [10] back soon. Goodbye." He did not tell them that ten workmen were cut off [11] from the shaft and that he wanted to go with the rescue squad. His wife suspected that it was worse than he had said, but she controlled herself and did not express her anxiety. "The poor man," she said. "Go quickly, but be careful, my dear."

1. Use *gern essen*. 2. Almost always sing. in German. 3. Not *essen*. 4. *kann unmöglich*. 5. Sing. 6. Insert *so*. 7. *gerade*. 8. Tr. "has happened." 9. *hoffentlich*. 10. Use present tense. 11. *ab*.

23. THE TRAVELLING JOURNEYMAN

Long before the rise of [1] trade unions every craftsman belonged to a guild. After an apprentice had completed his training he became a journeyman. It was the custom in Germany at that time for a journeyman to travel around from town to town before he perhaps became a [2] Master himself. These travelling journeymen were for the Romantics the symbol of the desire to travel and see the world [3] and of longing. One day one of these travelling journeymen was striding gaily through a great forest. He had risen before dawn and was now very hungry. When therefore he caught sight of a house in a clearing he went up to it [4] to beg or to buy his dinner. The door stood open and inside [5] he could see a table on which knife, fork, spoon, and bread lay beside a steaming plate. He knocked and waited, but not a sign of life, not even a dog. Finally the temptation was too strong. He went boldly to the table, sat down and began to eat. After he had wiped the last drop of gravy from the plate with a piece of bread, he made himself comfortable in a chair in front of the stove and, because he was tired, he at once fell asleep. It was late in the [6] afternoon when he awoke. To his surprise there was still no-one stirring in the house. He went for a stroll round the house and the little garden and then came back to the living room. There stood the table, laid and ready for supper again. As he was a bold fellow who was not easily intimidated, he once more fell to with a will.[7] "It has grown too late to travel further today," he said. "Perhaps there is a bed for me upstairs, too. But for the moment I am staying in this comfortable chair." Dusk was falling [8] already and gradually even he began to be rather frightened. The trees seemed to creep nearer in the gloom and he started at each small sound. After a time he could stand it no longer. "Rather walk the whole night than stay here in this bewitched house." When he stood again on the path he looked back at [9] the house and saw that a lamp now shone in the empty room he had left in darkness. With a cry of horror he broke into a run [10] and did not stop until [11] the house was quite out of sight.

    1. Def. Art. needed. 2. omit "a." **3.** *Wanderlust* adequately translates both phrases together. 4. *darauf zu.* 5. *drinnen.* 6. *am.* 7. *wacker.* 8. *es dämmerte.* 9. Prep? 10. Tr. "began to run." 11. Use *erst, als,* omitting "not."

24. THE GARDENER

Tom was our gardener. My friendship with him lasted many years, but it was divided into [1] two parts, for there was an interval of four or five years when it did not interest me to watch him at [2] his slow and patient work. He called me a naughty boy then, who spoilt or broke everything [3] he touched, and drove me out of the garden. When I was little I used to follow him round as he dug and planted. When he took the wheelbarrow he let me clamber on to it, and then I pretended it was a bus or a train as it trundled down the paths. In those days [4] wheelbarrows had no rubber tyres and it was an uncomfortable trip which I prized very highly all the same as a [5] reward and privilege. When Tom was setting out young flower or vegetable plants I was sometimes allowed [6] to help. I was never able to do it properly, for I was too much [7] afraid of injuring [8] the plants. Tom always said very politely to me, "Thank you, Adam." Then he would devise some excuse to get rid of me so that he could put everything to rights. He pressed the earth down hard with his great thumbs or even trod it down with his foot, and the plants flourished. The whole summer through the garden was full of bright flowers, but secretly he preferred vegetables. When he carried a basket full of peas or a massive cauliflower to the kitchen his face shone with [9] pride and pleasure. "Just [10] look at that, Adam," he would say and hold out, say,[11] a large ripe gooseberry. "Did you ever see such a beauty?" He did not wait for an answer, but popped [12] the berry into my mouth. It was always juicy and delicious, but I had to spit out the tough skin.

1. With Acc. 2. *bei*. 3. Add *was*. 4. *damals*. 5. Omit "a." 6. Use *dürfen* 7. *sehr* 8. Tr "that I should injure." 9. *vor*. 10. *mal*. 11. *etwa*. 12. *stecken*.

25. THE DIARY

After my father's death the sad duty of emptying his desk and burning his papers fell to me. I was his only son, my mother had been dead for years and the few relatives lived so scattered that there was nothing else for it [1] but to have most of the furniture [2] sold by auction. I had room [3] at home only for a few of the [4] pieces which I could not bear to see in the hands of strangers. I took as many of the books as my wife would allow and among these I discovered one day a volume of which my father was himself the author. Although bound it was in manuscript and when I had read it I understood why publication was not to be thought of, at least until all the people who were mentioned in it were dead. I knew that my father had always admired the diaries of Pepys but I did not know that he had found the time to keep [5] a journal of his own, for a doctor seldom has much leisure. On the other hand he is in a position to learn a great deal about his patients which is hidden from [6] their friends and I must admit that I laughed without restraint at many of the incidents he described. But there was tragedy as well as comedy on this stage and I found examples of [7] selfless courage which were described with a sympathy perhaps unexpected in a man whose profession brings him constantly into necessary contact with misfortune, sickness and death. It surprised me to learn [8] how often a doctor has thrust upon him the role of [7] adviser, confessor, and priest.

1. Use *nichts übrig bleiben*. 2. Use pl. because *das Möbel* is only one piece of furniture. 3. (*der*) *Platz*. 4. *einige*. 5. *führen*. 6. *vor*. 7. Tr. "of a." 8. *erfahren*.

26. AN OLD-FASHIONED SMITH

A choking cloud of blue [1] smoke arose and hid the stooping figure of the smith as he placed the glowing iron on the hoof held on the leathern apron between his knees. The horse stood patiently on three legs while the horseshoe was fastened on by means of long nails. Then the smith straightened his back and spoke. "When I learned this trade," he said, "there would have been three or four other horses standing outside. Nowadays —at the most two a [2] day. The horse has been crowded off the roads; he has lasted longer on the fields, but one tractor can do more work than a team of horses and even the ploughman does not need to walk.[3] Tractors don't come to me for [4] repair but to the garage down yonder. Two of those great tyres cost as much as a horse did [5] when I was a boy." "But you still have work." "They bring me these," said the smith, pointing to a plough, some chains and other agricultural implements lying on the ground, "but it isn't much and I have no apprentice who can follow me when I die. There was a time when [6] the smithy was the most important house in the village, except perhaps the inn. There must be thousands and thousands [7] of people whose surnames prove it, but," he shrugged his shoulders, "soon the origin of the name won't even strike them. It's old-fashioned we are and when the old smithy falls silent, when this fire that has burned for nigh on four hundred years finally goes out, only a few people like yourself will be sorry."

1. Adj. ending? 2. *am.* 3. To make this clear add *zu Fuss.* 4. *zur.* 5. Tr. "cost." 6. *wo.* 7. *tausend und abertausend.*

27. CONVALESCENCE

From the deck-chair on which he sat in the shade of the big pine tree Frederick had a wonderful view out over [1] the bay. He was not by nature lazy but his severe [2] illness had weakened him, and during [3] convalescence one is content to rediscover the world by looking at it. [4] So he had no desire to open the books which lay beside him. A rug covered his knees and it was pleasantly warm. The roses and the flower beds full of flowers whose names were unknown to him pleased him and the sound of the pigeons above his head was a peaceful accompaniment to his thoughts. A movement in the foliage drew his attention. Had he been well and busy he would just have said to himself, "a squirrel"—that is, if he had noticed it at all. But now it gave him pleasure to watch the brisk movements of the little animal with the big, bushy tail. It ran and jumped and was scarcely still for [5] a moment. Then suddenly it was gone. [6] Red ants climbed in an endless procession up and down the trunk, but it wearied him to watch them: they were so monotonously industrious, the personification of a virtue which he could not for the moment imitate. Gradually the buzzing of the insects and bees, the rustling of the pine branches, the summer [7] scents and the warmth numbed his senses. His eyes closed and half awake, half asleep,[8] he waited patiently for the end of the day.

1. *über hinaus*. 2. *schwer*. 3. Art. needed. 4. Omit "at it." 5. Omit "for." 6. *weg*. 7. Form Adj. with "-lich." 8. Tr. "half waking, half sleeping."

28. BIRTHDAY IN LONDON

LONDON

24th June

MY DEAR ELSBETH,

Today I didn't wake up until [1] half past eight, although I had expected that on [2] the first day of my stay in London the early buses and taxis would wake me much too early. But—half past eight—I am ashamed! It was the result of a very exciting but very exhausting day yesterday. I shall [3] soon be home again and then I will [3] describe everything to you in detail. You will envy me! In the first place it was my birthday and I was allowed to choose, except for the evening which was already arranged and was to remain a secret. So in [2] the morning I cashed the cheque I had as a present from Daddy and then went hunting for something pretty. Incidentally,[4] of course, I had a good look at half the biggest shops. I bought a pretty bracelet. In the afternoon we had a trip in a little steamer up the Thames to Kew. While we were eating ices [5] and cake they told

me that seats had been booked for the opera—Mozart's
Marriage of Figaro. You know how I adore Mozart's
music and it was a wonderful performance. We sat in [6]
the best seats. I don't really like to sit so near to the
stage that you can see the actors' make-up, but after
all the whole thing is only make believe,[7] isn't it? We
could understand every word without any difficulty and
it was fun to see the conductor from so near. I was
thrilled!

The holidays will [3] soon be over, but I am looking
forward to seeing you again soon.

With love from [8]

SOPHIE

1. Use *erst*. 2. Prep? 3. Use the present tense. 4. *dabei*.
5. Sing. 6. *auf*. 7. *Theater*. 8. *Es grüsst Dich recht herzlich*.

29. OUT SHOOTING

I had the impression that I had just [1] fallen asleep
when I was awakened and a cup of coffee was thrust
into my hands so that I should not go to sleep again.
"Put on plenty of [2] warm clothes and please be ready in
five minutes." Yawning and miserable, I got dressed
and went out of the house. The hot coffee, however,
had warmed me up and this, for me, new experience
began gradually to appear less foolish. "We will not
talk on the way," said my friend, "otherwise the animals
will hear us coming. Then we should have wasted our
time. We must make a long detour, too, so that they
don't scent us." After an hour had elapsed it began to
grow light and my friend signed to me to walk on the
pine needles at the edge of the track. Soon we were at
our destination and we stayed hidden behind a bush at

the forest edge. Before us lay an open field. The smaller birds were twittering in the forest and now and again we heard the harsh laugh of a jay or the cry of a magpie. While we were waiting I observed the gun my friend was holding under his arm. It was at the same time a shot-gun and a sporting rifle, for it had three barrels of which the third lay beneath the other two. I knew that guns of this kind are popular among [3] German sportsmen,[4] for in Germany deer are comparatively common. If one has a so called "triplet" with one, one is armed against game of every kind, be it deer or hare, pheasant or partridge, for two barrels are for small shot and the third for rifle bullets. Slowly and carefully the gun was raised and I saw now that a few deer had slipped out of the forest. They were feeding, quite unsuspecting, at [5] a distance of thirty metres. My friend took aim and fired.

1. *gerade.* 2. Use *viel.* Ending of following Adj. with plural noun? 3. *unter.* 4. *Jäger.* 5. *in.*

30. THE STORM

When you live on [1] the coast you are used to storms, but this wind was something out of the ordinary even here. It shrieked and howled like a madman and the waves beating [2] against the cliffs thundered continuously in the background although the beach was half a mile away. The bare branches of the trees near the farmhouse swayed wildly against the streaming grey clouds, and dead and broken wood lay scattered on the ground. Fortunately the animals were all in their stalls, for it was impossible to stand upright against the thrust of the wind for it caught hold of everything loose, everything it could move, and swept it away.[3] Two hen houses on

wheels which stood in a meadow in front of the farmhouse had been pushed as far as the wall, and when the
wind changed direction slightly [4] had toppled over.
Every door and [5] window in the house rattled although
it was in a little valley and thus sheltered from the full
force of the gale.[6] Small pebbles and twigs were thrown
like rain against the panes, but in spite of the noise very
little damage was done.[7] From the news on the [8] radio,
however, we learned that not very far away it was very
different.[9] The strong wind behind the already high
tide had formed gigantic waves which had broken
through the dykes and had flooded the streets of many
seaside towns.

1. *an.* 2. Use *schlagen.* 3. *fort.* 4. Tr. "a little." 5. "door"
and "window" are not the same gender. Tr. "all the." 6.
Tr. "storm." 7. *angerichtet.* 8. *im.* 9. *ganz anders.*

SECOND YEAR

31. THE VILLAGE SHOP

At the entrance to the village stands a shop, no, "the" shop, for there is no other. Over the display window hangs a sign bearing the name "W. J. Brown." Nothing more. Not "Groceries," not "Chemist" nor "Drapers," for this shop is all three at once,[1] and more, too, for it is the Post Office and contains the only telephone in the village. The owner, manager, and saleswoman is an elderly but very cheerful and vigorous lady, a widow by the name of[2] Domaney, née Brown. Her father lies upstairs in bed. He is cared for[3] by his other, the unmarried daughter, who keeps house also for her sister. Naturally there are things that cannot be bought in the shop, bread for example, meat and fish. These are delivered from the town twice a week, and if you need anything expensive or large you take[4] the bus to the town. Of course you do that too if you are only seeking an excuse for an afternoon in the town, but if you need anything from soap powder to a picture postcard, you can find it here. You must[5] not be in a hurry for Mrs Domaney knows the gossip and the rumours like no other lady in the village. But she is not in the least malicious. On the contrary she is most kind-hearted and will help if she can. However[6] stormy the night may be, no telegram has ever had to wait till morning. Off[7] she goes on her bicycle and you cannot take it amiss if she says, "Bad news, I'm afraid,"[8] or "It's a boy. Congratulations!"

1. Tr. "all in one." 2. *namens*. 3. Make this active. 4. Tr. "go by," *fahren mit*. 5. Use *dürfen*. 6. *wie . . . auch immer*. 7. *fort*. 8. *leider*.

32. THE HERMIT

At the edge of the forest stood a tumbledown old house. I first [1] saw it one day when I was looking for mushrooms. With its thatched roof and whitewashed walls it must once [2] have been very picturesque. Now, however, both gables were crooked and the whole structure was full of holes. In some places the roof was completely missing and part of the attic stood open to the sky and the rain. I stepped through a gap in the fence, but as I came nearer two white goats appeared out of a barn and trotted bleating towards me. At once an indignant voice cried, "Have you let those dratted goats loose?" the house door opened and an old man rushed out. Without another word [3] he seized the largest animal and tugged and dragged it back into the shed. The smaller goat ran along behind [4] and all three disappeared. I would have liked to assert my innocence, but the old man had looked so angry that I went on my way.[5] When I reached the village I drank a glass of excellent beer in the inn and learned that the old man whom I had encountered lived quite alone in his cottage. His wife, who now lived with [6] a son-in-law, had refused to endure the conditions any [7] longer, for, apart from the miserable condition of the house itself, the well was usually dry and every drop of water had to be carried a hundred yards. There he lived, the old chap, 73 years of age [8] and determined to die [9] where he had always lived. They called him the hermit and considered him a little mad.

1. Tr. "for the first time." 2. *einst*, or *früher*. 3. Add *zu sagen*. 4. along behind—*hinterher*. 5. *meines Weges*. 6. *bei*. 7. Omit "any." 8. Tr. "old." 9. Insert *dort* or *da*.

33. THE MESSENGER

The rider pulled hard on the reins and forced his foam-flecked horse to a halt on the river bank. He swore loudly. The peasant had been right and he had not believed him. The bridge was indeed blown and the river was too wide and the current too strong for [1] him to swim across. He had to make a decision quickly. Were all the bridges from here to the mouth of the river destroyed? And if he went further upstream would he fall into the hands of the enemy? The longer [2] he waited the more [2] dangerous the situation became. Victory or defeat might [3] depend on the news he carried. He struck spurs into his horse's belly and galloped northwards. There was a ferry not far away and perhaps it had been overlooked in the hurried retreat. He lessened his speed, leaped through a gap in the hedge and rode through the meadows to avoid the detour where road and river no longer ran together through the valley. Soon he was in the sunken road which led to the ferry. Thank heavens, the boat was there. He dismounted, untied the boat and rowed across. The horse neighed loudly and plunged into the water. Without a rider on its back it had just [4] enough strength still to [5] swim. On the other side it stood quivering and steam rose from its panting body while a sword thrust made a hole in the planks of the boat. Then on, but more slowly now, for the horse was nearly exhausted and the worst was overcome. The goal was almost in sight.

1. *als dass.* 2. *je . . . desto.* 3. Use *können.* 4. *gerade.*
5. *zum Schwimmen.*

34. SPRING IN [1] THE COUNTRY

At last he could work no longer. He rose from his desk,[2] took his walking stick and went out of the house. He had come into [1] the country because he wanted to write the last chapters of his book, but it was even more difficult here than in the town, for the lovely spring weather distracted his thoughts. It was the middle of April [3] and birds sang from [4] every hedge and thicket. As he walked now past [5] the orchard there seemed to be a thrush or a blackbird on every branch, and from the neighbouring wood a cuckoo called monotonously. The blossom of cherry, plum, and pear hung like a white cloud against the blue of the sky. In every garden there were wallflowers and tulips and even the despised dandelion made pretty yellow patches in the fresh green of the meadows. The path now led him into a wood where the buds of the beeches formed a green veil over the smooth grey trunks. Here all was cool and still and the scent of dead [6] leaves which rustled beneath his feet was strong. But that was material for a lyric poet and poetry did not concern him, at least not while other work was waiting. His publisher expected his detective story at the latest before the end of the month. Reluctantly he returned to his desk.

1. *Auf.*   2. Not *Pult* here, but *Schreibtisch.*   3. *Mitte April.* 4. *in.*   5. *an . . . vorbei.*   6. *welk.*

35. THE BEGINNING OF THE HOLIDAYS

On the evening before the journey we could never go to sleep. Every year it was the same. Then we got up too early and got in Mother's way while the last things were being packed. At last the taxi arrived, the luggage was carried out of the house and we got in. My father never went with us. There were [1] he said, various things to see to in the factory and he would meet us later at the station; besides there was [1] no room in the taxi. When I understood later that all this was only an excuse I found it selfish but in reality [2] he was probably quite right, for he would only have been even more in the way than us. At the station there was always at least half an hour to wait, but it was a big station and we had to find the right platform. The tickets had been bought in advance. The luggage was carried away by a porter, who also selected an empty compartment for us, for which Mother rewarded him with a large tip. Father always arrived at the very last [3] moment, but this time it looked as though he had overdone it and would miss the train. We leaned out of [4] the window and gazed anxiously towards the barrier. When he came in sight the train was beginning to move. He just had time to jump into the last carriage and he soon appeared in the corridor. "All's well that ends well," [5] he said.

1. Mood? 2. *im Grunde genommen*. 3. *allerletzt*. 4. *zum . . . hinaus*. 5. *Ende gut, alles gut*.

36. IN THE FOG

I was on the road which runs over the moor when I ran [1] into the fog, not gradually, but [2] as suddenly as though I had run [1] into a thick cloud. The headlights lit up the fog and reduced the visibility still further. So [3] I switched them off and, leaning [4] out of the window, I followed the white posts which stood on both sides of the road. For five minutes I went [1] slowly forwards, then the engine stuttered a few times [5] and was dumb.

With the aid of an electric torch I looked for the cause
of the breakdown—I had no petrol. I knew that the
last bus had passed an hour ago and it was now so late
that it would be an unusual stroke of luck if a car should
find me. There were only two possibilities. Either I
could sit in the car until [6] daylight brought the first
traffic, or I could walk to the next village. I had soon
made up my mind, for I should be able to walk almost as
fast as I had previously [7] been driving in the fog. As so
often happens in such a fog on the moor, the sky was
clearly visible. After a time when I looked up [8] I suddenly noticed that the moon, which had at first been on
my left,[9] now stood straight ahead.[10] I was well acquainted with the district and I knew that the road was
dead straight. I must have turned left down one of the
side-roads. To reach the nearest village in this direction,
I should have to walk all night.

1. Use "drive." 2. *aber* or *sondern*? 3. When "so" means
"and so, therefore," it is better not to put it first in the German
sentence. 4. *gelehnt*. 5. *ein paar Male* and *ein paarmal* are both
correct. 6. Def. Art. required. 7. *vorher*. 8. *hinauf*. 9. *zu
meiner Linken*. 10. *vor mir*.

37. THE FIRE

When the fire brigade arrived the flames were already
shooting out of a first-floor window [1] and it looked as
though they could do no more than protect the neighbouring buildings. In such cases the sympathies of the
crowd are always on the side of [2] the fire, provided that
no-one is in danger, and there were rumours enough
circulating that the owner himself was not exactly inconsolable. Better an adequate compensation from the
insurance than a bankrupt business that no-one would
buy. But the older men [3] shook their heads [4] sadly.

They thought of the days [5] when Hinker and Company had been one of the best firms in the town. Old [6] Hinker was a hard-working, capable business man and had fully deserved the honour of being elected mayor. The elder son, his successor, was a chip of the old block but he had unfortunately been killed [7] in the war and one had to admit that young [6] William was nothing more than a pleasure-seeking good-for-nothing. Since he had almost succumbed to a severe illness in his early childhood his late mother had always spoiled him, and under his slack administration the business had gone to rack and ruin. The whole town knew that the firm was on its last legs. This fire had come at too convenient a time not to arouse [8] suspicion. The crowd expected [9] the roof to fall in at any moment but to the general astonishment that did not happen. On the contrary the flames had disappeared within a short space of time. "Bad luck," said a voice in the crowd and everyone laughed.

1. Tr. "window on the first floor." 2. *auf Seiten* (with Gen.). 3. *Herren.* 4. Sing. 5. Tr. "time." 6. Affectionately or familiarly the Def. Art. is added before the Adj. 7. Tr. "had fallen." 8. Tr. "to arouse no. . . ." 9. Tr. "That . . . would. . . ."

38. JOAN ASKS FOR HELP

Joan came up through the garden instead of going up the drive to the front door. She already knew the Grants [1] well enough for that [2] and she knew, too, that they did not like it if their friends stood at the door ringing the bell "like strangers paying a call." They made no fuss themselves and visitors who took offence were making a great mistake, for no family could have been so helpful and kind-hearted in things that mattered.[3] In this house they were apparently always busy, yet the family was always ready to let the guest help with any activity, whether it was a matter of bottling fruit or solving the cross-word puzzle. Joan remembered her first visit and smiled. She had found herself up [4] on a ladder picking [5] apples before she had been introduced to Mr and Mrs Grant. She had met Kathleen two months ago at the tennis club and had quickly made friends with her. A way of life that other people might have found unbearable seemed to her warm and friendly. It was perhaps due to this contrast with her life at home with her stepmother that she valued her friendship with this family so highly. She stepped on to the veranda and Kathleen's voice called from her bedroom, "Just [6] coming, Joan. Play the [7] piano if you want to. I will be [8] there in five minutes." There seemed [9] to be something on every chair, a cat or some knitting or a book, so she sat down at the piano, but she did not play. She thought of the time since her mother's death. She could stand it no longer. She must escape and find a fresh [10] life. That was the reason for her visit this afternoon. She wanted to discuss her plans with Kathleen, for her friend was sensible and would consider the situation calmly, without dismay and without reproaches.

1. Omit "the" or say *Familie Grant*. 2. *dazu*. 3. Tr. "when it was a matter of something important (*wichtig*)." 4. *oben*. 5. *bei* with verbal noun. 6. *gleich*. 7. Omit "the." 8. Use present tense. 9. Tr. "there was apparently." 10. Tr. "new."

39. ON CHRISTMAS EVE

I came out of the station and for the first time began to doubt whether I should get to Steepleton at all. The snow here in the country was clearly very different from

the London [1] snow, which was unpleasant but nothing
more. In [2] reply to my inquiry, "The next bus to
Steepleton. Tomorrow perhaps—that is, if it doesn't
snow again. On the main roads it is not so bad, but you
won't get to Steepleton today unless you walk.[3] I am
sorry, Sir." I had travelled 100 miles to celebrate
Christmas with [4] my uncle and aunt and it would have
annoyed me beyond all measure to spend it [5] in an inn
only four miles away from them. I was sorry that I had
not sent my presents on in advance by [4] post, but even
if I had [6] they would probably not have got there in [4]
this weather. I had no desire to lug my heavy case
through the deep snow, so I unpacked a few things, a
razor and a toothbrush, and put them in my pocket.
The rest I could borrow from my uncle or from my
cousin if he was not away. Then I handed in my case at
the station and set out. As soon as I was out of the town
I was glad that I had to walk, for the scene [7] was one of
dazzling beauty. I had often gone this way in summer,
but everything had become unrecognizable now. The
mantle of snow covered every landmark and made [8]
the familiar seem strange and new. At first I gazed
around me with curiosity; I saw the tracks of animals,
noticed how yellow the sheep looked against the white
fields, but after half an hour the eternal white hurt my
eyes. The snowdrifts were deep and I constantly had
to turn aside from the road and go through the fields.
This was extremely tiring, for the ditches were invisible,
and I stumbled and fell [9] a hundred times.

1. Adj. formed from place names are invariable. 2. *Als.*
3. To make this clear, add *zu Fuss.* 4. Prep? 5. Tr. *das Fest.*
6. Add "done it." 7. *die Landschaft.* 8. Use *lassen.* 9. Add
hin.

40. THE ELM TREE

From my earliest childhood I harboured the desire [1] to climb the big tree at the end of our garden. It was a huge elm tree, at least 80 feet high in whose topmost branches a number of rooks used to build their untidy nests. Most trees have a roughly circular or triangular shape, but like all elms this tree was recognizable by its lack of symmetry. Around its base [2] stood a small thicket of elm shoots, but no branches formed a ladder up the trunk. Not until [3] I was fourteen did I make a serious attempt to conquer my private Everest. I had found a rope and after repeated failure I succeeded in throwing one end over the lowest large branch. After fastening both ends I swarmed [4] up and the first and most difficult obstacle was overcome. From there on [5] the tree was like any other, only by far the biggest I had climbed, till at [6] a height of 60 feet it became impossible to climb any [7] further. I stayed there for a while to enjoy the unusual view. Then I made the descent. When I described my exploit to my parents at supper and said that for once there were no nests in the elm tree, my father was very angry. I had to promise never to climb an elm again. They were very dangerous, he said. Not until [3] two years later did I see that he was right, for during a storm the great elm crashed down in our garden and we could see that the trunk was hollow and rotten.

1. Tr. "wish." 2. Tr. "foot." 3. Use *erst.* 4. Tr. "climbed." 5. *an.* 6. *in.* 7. Omit "any."

41. THE TRAMP

He looked as though he had not eaten anything for a week but he accepted our bread and cheese with dignity and only on [1] condition that we found him some [2] work to do afterwards. "I prefer to earn my daily bread," he said as he began to eat. His voice showed that he was an educated man, his worn out clothes were of [3] good material and he wore shoes, not the heavy boots one would have expected. He even wore a tie with diagonal stripes of the kind that have a significance for those who are able to decipher it. When he took off his hat one could see that he had recently been at [4] the barber's. All in all, a strange tramp. As an [5] honest, hard-working citizen I could not regard such an able-bodied unemployed man [6] with approval. Today at any rate he should work for a change although it was Sunday. I indicated a long neglected hedge. "Will you clip that for me?" I said. "With pleasure," he replied. The children fetched the necessary tools and I returned to my own work. I must admit that I completely forgot him and I was surprised to find him again in [7] the evening. He looked extremely tired, and no wonder, for I had set him a task that I had been avoiding for weeks myself. My conscience smote [8] me and I offered him supper. He accepted again, thanked me with gentle courtesy and asked if he might [9] spend the night in the barn. I felt a mixture of curiosity, envy and disapproval. I wanted to interrogate him, but I could not do it. I could not behave with less courtesy than a tramp.

---

1. *unter der.*   2. Omit "some."   3. *aus.*   4. *bei.*   5. Omit "an."   6. Use "unemployed" as noun.   7. Prep?   8. Tr. "had remorse."   9. Use *dürfen.*

42. IN THE CASTLE

The voice of the guide reciting facts, and adding now and then a joke that he had been making on the same spot for 25 years, paused for a moment and the obedient little procession moved on.[1] John stayed behind to[2] linger on the wall. He hoped that no-one had noticed,[3] for he did not want to offend the official, who was carrying out his duties[4] with patience and skill, but he wanted atmosphere,[5] not facts. That was why he had always had "unsatisfactory" for history at school. He loved[6] ruins, old castles and the like, the older the better. It delighted him to look at what[7] was left of a staircase or a fireplace and to imagine what life really was like[8] in those days. Could the man who lived there nearly a thousand years ago be compared with modern man? Was it sheer vanity if one believed that all the changes in the outward circumstances of his life have had some effect on his mind, his feelings? But the same thoughts probably passed through the head of the soldier standing guard up here on the wall, and of his brother who was in the trenches[9] during the World War. That the former carried a crossbow and the latter a rifle made no difference. Scientific discoveries had touched only the surface of life. Fundamentally, the problems, the hopes[9] and the fears[9] remained the same. "Birth and the grave, an eternal sea," the Earth Spirit in Goethe's *Faust* had called it.

1. *weiter*. 2. *um . . . zu*. 3. Add "it." 4. Sing. 5. This can be stressed by putting it in front of "he wanted." 6. *schwärmte für*. 7. *das, was*. 8. *wie . . . war*. 9. Sing.

43. LONDON

It is strange how different the same place can look at various times or under different circumstances without having changed in the least. For instance, a building we knew well during our childhood always seems [1] to be so much smaller when we return after a long absence. Disappointment lies in wait when you visit a second time the scene of some great happiness. Something is always missing and the magic cannot be [2] revived. Often, of course, it depends on mood. London has this effect on me. Usually I love London and consider it the finest capital in Europe. But sometimes I hate it. The centre seems [1] noisy, superficial and heartless, and the whole thing [3] is too big and too full of people who know nothing of one another. A crazy anthill covered with television aerials and full of newspapers in place of ideas and feelings.

These were my thoughts one day in the train and my expression must have shown my disgust, for the only other traveller in the compartment laughed and asked me whether I had swallowed something unpleasant.[4] "Yes," I answered, "London." His accent was foreign and I regretted my rudeness so I explained what I meant. He told me he could well understand, for he came from a country whose total population was only one third of the number of inhabitants of London. He said a little sadly that it was strange how lonely one could be among [5] so many people. He was a cultured and interesting man and that was the beginning of a friendship that has lasted ten years.

1. Use *vorkommen*.   2. *lässt sich nicht*.   3. *das Ganze*.   4. Capital letter for Adj. used as Noun.   5. *unter, mitten unter*.

44. THE VISIT

"How infinitely kind to invite me so soon," thought Jane, "and to send her own carriage besides to fetch me, although my mother was after all only a distant relative of the Duchess." As the carriage drove through the village street with harness jingling, the village folk saluted respectfully and Jane felt for the first time in her life how advantageous it might be to live, as it were,[1] under [2] the shadow of a noble coat of arms. Jane was not ambitious to play a great role in society, and wealth did not dazzle her, but for the daughter of a poor widow the present circumstances naturally aroused pleasant speculation. High iron gates were opened wide as they approached [3] and a smiling woman curtseyed, thinking [4] no doubt the Duchess was behind the sunshade. The house [5] was to be seen now and again between the chestnut trees of the avenue and the spectacle filled the young visitor [6] with wonder. She had never seen so large a building. The façade was in [7] the classical fashion which houses of this size are obliged [8] to adopt, and although the right angles and pillars did not suit the English landscape they were extremely elegant and distinguished. Before Jane had time to fall from admiration into nervousness the carriage reached the house and she heard her name announced.

1. *gleichsam.* 2. Tr. "in." 3. Tr. "at their approach." 4. Tr. "in the belief." 5. Use *Schloss.* 6. There is no feminine form for *Gast.* 7. *nach.* 8. Use *zwangsweise.*

45. THE DOCKS

I had never been down [1] to the docks before. Naturally, I had often spent my holidays by [2] the sea, I had crossed the Channel several times but that was not the same. At a seaside resort or on a small passenger ship everything is arranged for the comfort and convenience of the visitors or passengers. This large port was the sea in shirt sleeves; the sight of it brought it home to you that England is still an island, a country that must import vast quantities of raw materials or [3] starve. It seemed a hopeless undertaking to look for a particular ship's captain amid this turmoil. But it was not so difficult after all.[4] I had been told the number of the wharf and quite soon [5] I found myself on the gangway leading onto the deck of the ship I was seeking. Huge bales were being hoisted from gaping holds on the end of doubtful looking wire ropes which dangled from the top of tall cranes. The rattle of machines and the sound of human voices shouting incomprehensible orders filled the air. Down in his cabin I found the captain at his desk. He was busy [6] tidying up a great heap of papers. As I entered he looked up, rose, and offered me his hand. "I am glad you have come, Mr Johannis. I hope you have brought the money with [7] you?"

1. Omit "down." 2. *an.* 3. *um nicht zu.* 4. Put "after all" earlier in the sentence. 5. Tr. "quickly." 6. Add *damit.* 7. Omit "you."

46. THE MISSED TRAIN

Time was pretty short when the train moved slowly into the terminus. We were a quarter of an hour late and my connection left in half a minute. I reached my case and mackintosh down from the rack and waited with [1] my hand on the door handle for the train to stop. Then I leaped on to the platform and raced for the barrier. No use. The express had left on time. So I had three and a half [2] hours to wait. I handed my

luggage in at the left luggage office and rang up my
client from a public telephone box. What was to be
done now? I had no desire to spend three hours in a
waiting room, no cinema was open in the morning. It
was hopeless to look for anything worth seeing in this
little town for it was only of importance as a [3] railway
junction. I strolled unhappily out into the ugly streets
prepared to enter the first public house I saw.[4] Then
from the distance I heard the unmistakable sound of a
fair. I went in the direction of the music and when I
reached the town hall there was the square full of stalls,
roundabouts, and spectators. Towering [5] above it all
was the tall framework of a scenic railway. Entertain-
ments of this kind [6] are of course best in the evening, but
even in broad [7] daylight they attract, particularly when
you have absolutely nothing else [8] to do. I got rid of
two hours and all my small change before I turned away.
On the way back to the station I was still smiling at [9]
the ridiculous nonsense that the fortune teller had
dished up to me. The culmination was that today was a
lucky day for me. And I had missed my train and a
valuable piece of business was perhaps lost!

But she was right. The train I had missed had been
derailed and ten people had lost their lives.

1. Omit "with." 2. *dreieinhalb* (invar.) (*Stunden*) or *drei und
eine halbe* (*Stunde*). 3. Omit "a." 4. first I saw—*das erste beste.*
5. Tr. ". . . railway towered above it all." 6. *solche* or *der-
artige.* 7. *hell.* 8. *sonst.* 9. *über.*

47. TWO FRIENDS

At the same hour every day two friends were to be
seen in the park and when you encountered them for the
first time you were compelled to take a sudden interest

in some [1] flower bed in order to hide your [2] smile. Not only were both of them rather comical in themselves,[3] but together they presented a complete contrast in appearance and, so far as one could judge, in [4] character. The one was very tall and thin, with a pale, clean-shaven face, sharp pointed nose and high cheek-bones. He was always dressed in the same way, regardless of the weather. He wore a black or dark grey suit with unusually narrow trousers, a high stiff collar, which threatened to cut his chin each time he turned his head, and a bowler hat. On his hands he always had yellow gloves and he carried a tightly rolled umbrella which he did not use as a walking stick but carried on his arm. A sombre, somewhat sinister figure. His companion was quite different. He was short and fat, with a red face that shone with good nature and health. He always wore something colourful,[5] a tie, or a silk handkerchief in his breast pocket, or a flower in his buttonhole. Where the other was restrained and gloomy, he was boisterous and affable. He talked very loudly and waved his arms about to emphasize his words. Sometimes they sat for a while on a bench. The thin man sat very stiff and straight and seldom raised his eyes from the ground. The fat man lay comfortably back, placed his hat on his knees and stared calmly at the people passing by.[6]

1. *irgend ein.* 2. Possessive of *man?* 3. *an sich.* 4. *an.* 5. Insert *etwa.* 6. People passing by—tr. by one word.

48. ALBRECHT DÜRER

Twelve years before the birth of Luther, the wife of a goldsmith in the town of [1] Nuremberg bore a son who became as famous as the "Father of the Reformation" and whose works contributed in a different way to the

religious life of his day.[2] Albrecht Dürer was an artist
and he told in pictures much [3] of the same story that
Luther made available to the German people in words.
The life and death of Christ [4] could be understood
even by those who could not read, when they saw them
in Dürer's woodcuts. It is a pity that Dürer did not
meet his great contemporary for he might have painted
a picture of him. The portrait of his mother is one of
Dürer's most interesting pictures, although it is a drawing
and not an oil painting. It portrays an old woman
whose face, full of strength and courage, shows what a
hard life she had led. The forehead is covered with
wrinkles, the nose juts out sharply between sunken
cheeks, and the eyes have the watchful expression of
one [5] who has suffered much, but whom life has not
embittered, and for whom death has no terrors.

Death himself is to be seen in one of his most famous
etchings—*The Knight, Death, and the Devil*—but he does
not use the figure of death as a symbol so frequently as
Holbein, who loved to remind us that death is always at
our [6] side.

1. Omit "of." 2. Tr. "time." 3. Tr. "a great part." 4.
Christi. 5. Tr. "of a person." 6. *an der; zur Seite* would mean
"in support."

49. THE SIEGE OF STRALSUND

On June 7, 1628, Lambert Steinwick, Mayor of
Stralsund, a little town [1] on the coast of Pomerania, was
in session with his anxious Corporation in the town hall.
"We have only 3000 men. How shall we resist much
longer the attacks of the Imperial Army which last year
drove King Christian of Denmark back into his islands?
For thirty days our people have shown the steadfastness

of hardened soldiers, but this siege can only end one way since [2] there are ten enemies to one defender. Twenty cannon bombard our walls without respite. After each attack we are weaker, with each hour we are less capable of repulsing the repeated assaults. When last [3] our delegates held a parley with Field-Marshal Arnim he offered surrender with honour. The haughty Wallenstein, who left the court at Prague not long ago,[4] will offer no such terms." An angry murmur followed this speech and another Councillor rose. "Wallenstein, Admiral of the Baltic," he quoted scornfully. "The Admiral without a fleet. Today that is a jest; but if Stralsund yields, every Hansa town will join the Imperial cause; the Baltic will become [5] a Habsburg lake. The Habsburgs, the Catholic oppressors. If that is not true, why has Wallenstein said: 'Stralsund must fall, were it hung by chains from Heaven'? We do not stand alone; at this very moment [6] 800 gallant Scots are landing from King Christian's ships under [7] the noses [8] of the enemy, who can do nothing to prevent it. Let us [9] take heart and speak no more of defeat or submission."

1. Case? 2. *da*. 3. Tr. "the last time." 4. *vor kurzem*. 5. *zu* is necessary here. 6. *eben jetzt*. 7. *vor*. 8. Sing. 9. Not *lassen*.

50. A YOUNG PRINCE

What would have been the possible consequences if some single, important historical event had ended differently? Historians on occasion play with such suppositions among themselves. If Napoleon, for example, had won the battle of Waterloo? What would have happened if Frederick, 18-year-old Crown Prince of Prussia, had succeeded [1] in his attempt [2] to flee from the tyrannical treatment of his father the King? The

attempt actually took place in the year 1730, during a
journey through Germany when Frederick intended [3]
to flee across the Dutch frontier and seek [4] sanctuary in
England. About two o'clock in the morning Frederick,
wearing a long red cloak, emerged from the barns in
which the King and his retinue were spending the night
and waited for [5] the horses which would have carried
him to [6] safety. The King knew, however, what his son
intended and two colonels and another officer had
received orders [7] not to let Frederick out of their sight.[8]
The flight was over even before it had begun. "You
treat me as a [9] slave, not as a [9] son," said Frederick to
his enraged father, who drew his sword and might have
slain the heir to the throne on the spot if an officer had
not placed himself in front of the culprit. The Prince
was arrested and sent to the fortress of Cüstrin, 60 miles
from Berlin. He and Lieut. Katte, his friend and
accomplice, appeared before a court martial. The
moderate sentence was rejected by the King who
personally passed sentence of death [10] on Katte.
Frederick stood at the window of the prison as his friend
passed by on his way to the scaffold, "My dear Katte,
forgive me," he cried and fell to the [11] ground in a swoon.

1. Use *gelingen* impersonally and watch agreement. 2. Tr.
"when he attempted." 3. *wollte.* 4. Add "a." 5. Prep?
6. *in.* 7. Sing. 8. *aus den Augen.* 9. Remember that *als*
identifies, *wie* compares. 10. One word. 11. Omit "the."

51. ON A SUMMER'S DAY [1]

Edward was not at [2] school, for his brother had
measles. Later, perhaps, he would have them, but for
the time being he was merely the carrier of an infectious
disease and had to work at home. It was such a glorious

day that it was impossible to sit at home alone with
one's [3] books. So he lay in the boat, a contented idler,
and the books which were to [4] satisfy his conscience
served him for [5] a pillow. For a while he tried to recall
the timetable so that [6] he might know what his friends
were doing in school, but thinking [7] made him tired.
There was no point in it [8] either. The boat rocked and
tugged gently at the rope which fastened it to a root in
the bank. Edward dipped his hand in the water and
lazily tried to catch leaves and pieces of wood as they
floated by. Since he was looking into the sky at the same
time it was no wonder that he caught nothing at all.
The clouds sailed slowly behind the branches of the
willow tree. Sometimes they kept the same shape when
they came into sight again, sometimes a castle had
changed into a sailing ship or a teapot. It was interesting
and made no demands on the mental faculties. When
he was tired of that he raised his head a little and watched
the swallows shooting to and fro above the water. They
were flying so quickly they couldn't possibly [9] be
hunting for insects. Probably they keep their beaks [10]
open and leave [11] the rest to chance, thought Edward.
Now and then a family of ducks swam by. The father,
or was it the mother?, looked very self-important, like a
destroyer escorting a convoy. When he threw bits of
bread into the water the birds steered towards them, [12]
examined and devoured the gift.

1. "Summer's day" one word. 2. *in der*. 3. Possessive of
man? 4. Use *sollen*. 5. *als*. 6. *um zu wissen*. 7. cf *das
Schwimmen*—swimming. 8. *Es hatte keinen Zweck*. 9. Tr. "could
impossibly." 10. Sing. as in "the boys raised their caps," etc.
11. *überlassen*. 12. *darauf los*.

52. IN THE AIR

"Fasten your safety belts, please." [1] Mr Shotter looked through the side window and saw the runway rushing by; then it disappeared; one no longer had any sensation of speed; they were in the air. Mr Shotter's hand automatically sought for his parachute and he smiled, for during the war he had served as a paratrooper; since then he had never been in an aeroplane. The arrival this time should be peaceful by comparison with many he had experienced which had been far from it. [2] Provided that no customs officials examined the brief-case he was carrying too carefully. But why should those [3] gentlemen concern themselves with papers? They were chiefly interested in jewels, scent, stockings and so on. Mr Shotter calmed himself and now began to enjoy his journey. It was much more comfortable on the upholstered seats in this civil plane than on the hard metal benches in the transport planes. With these jet engines one flew naturally much faster, but in many respects there was surprisingly little difference. He looked down again and admired the beauty of the clouds whose level surface gleamed like brilliant white cotton wool. Against these clouds the huge wing seemed to be quite motionless. It was incredible that it was in fact cutting through the air at a speed that would bring him to his destination in a few hours, while the ships which he could glimpse now and then through the clouds would need as many days to cover the same distance.

1. *Bitte, anschnallen.* 2. *alles andere gewesen waren.* 3. *jener* is comparatively rare, *dieser*, or in ordinary speech *der*, is more usual.

53. FREDERICK AND VOLTAIRE

Of Frederick the Great and Bismarck it can be said that they were the architects of modern Germany [1] which, twice within a generation, came near to [2] conquering all Europe, if not the whole world. Yet the former used his native tongue only in [3] addressing his servants and his soldiers. Macaulay describes him during the darkest days of the Seven Years War with a bottle of poison in one pocket and a bundle of his own verses in the other. The poems were in French. It is therefore the more interesting to note that the eyes of the German literary world turned away from France and towards England just at the time when Frederick sat on the Prussian throne. Lessing's famous attack on those German authors who aped French Classicism was published in 1759, only a few years after Voltaire left Berlin whither he had gone [4] in 1750 at [5] the urgent invitation of Frederick. The story of the friendship, if friendship it can be called, between the King and the rebel who was finally compelled to flee his own country, has given a perhaps unworthy malicious pleasure to many. Both were disappointed when they met, the one that a philosopher could be so grasping and the other that a King could be so petty. Frederick admired Voltaire as a writer even when he had come to [6] despise him as a man, but whether Voltaire for his part admired Frederick is extremely doubtful. After correcting Frederick's French verse for years he remarked that he was "tired of washing his dirty linen for him." Frederick was equally rude about Voltaire and it is no wonder that they quarrelled in a most unedifying manner.

1. Geographical names preceded by an Adj. have the Def. Art. and usually drop the Gen. "s." 2. *daran*. 3. Either *um . . . zu*, or *als er*. . . . 4. Use *sich begeben*. 5. Use *zufolge* with Dat. after the noun. 6. Tr. "had learned to."

54. GOOD ADVICE

He did not at once reply to my question, but stood gazing silently down into the garden where the colours were fading into the general grey of evening. Then he turned and I saw that he had forgotten my presence. "I beg your pardon," he said, "I was thinking of the past. Please sit down." He switched on the light, drew the curtains and sat down opposite me.

"You must not think me unsympathetic. That you ask me for advice is very flattering and I must admit that I should like to help you. After all, old people have more experience behind them than young people and it is a pity if we cannot pass on the fruits of that experience to others. We have all made mistakes, learned from them, and would willingly help others to avoid our own suffering and disappointment. But it is dangerous to assume that similar causes always produce the same results. The circumstances may indeed be identical, human beings never. Many a man has chosen a profession or has entered upon a career which to all appearances were quite unsuited to his abilities or his character. I know such people who have won happiness and even wealth. On the other hand there are people who have not succeeded in reaching either,[1] despite the most favourable opportunities. You are at the crossroads, my friend. You have to choose between dull security and the charm of the unknown. I am the more reluctant to express an opinion because forty years ago I had to choose myself. I, too, asked for advice, and regretted it ever since. No, I will tell you what I know, but the decision you must make for yourself."

1. Tr. "neither the one nor the other."

55. THE COLLISION

It was shortly after midnight when the accident happened. A dream in which all manner of events take place and which seems to last a long time, occupies in reality only the fraction of a second. In my dreams the earth was rocking under the shocks of an earthquake. I was running down the street while great cracks appeared everywhere and tiles flew through the air; but I was the only person who had noticed what was wrong [1] and I was yelling, "Come out, come out. The houses are going to collapse," when I awoke. I stared out through the porthole into the night and saw what I took to be the reflection of the light on the fog outside. Suddenly a face appeared and we both recoiled in mutual astonishment, for one does not expect to gaze into a lighted cabin only a few yards away in the middle of the Atlantic. There was a tremendous din, drowned at regular intervals by the deep moaning of the fog-horn. When I reached the deck sailors were hurrying to and fro and in the bows powerful searchlights lit up the figures of men working with ropes and planks. No time had been wasted.[2] One of the ship's officers had even found time to explain to the group of passengers, to which I had attached myself, what had happened. Another ship had suddenly appeared out of the fog and a collision had been inevitable, but thanks to the helmsman the damage was not so great as it might have been.[3] There was a gaping hole in the side of our ship, but it was well [4] above the water and there was no further danger in [5] this calm weather.

1. *los.* 2. Tr. "had been lost." 3. verb order? 4. Tr. "far." 5. *bei.*

56. "OLD FRITZ"

When Frederick returned from the campaigns of the Seven Years War in 1763 he still had 23 years of his life before him,[1] that is to say exactly the same length of time [2] that he had already spent as King. The country he ruled had, at [3] his accession, been a new and unimportant kingdom; now it stood in the front [4] rank of European powers. But in order to effect this change Frederick had had to sacrifice everything that his forbears had amassed in the past hundred years. Silesia he had indeed [5] won and held, but, for all that,[6] Prussia was utterly devastated and impoverished. With the same ruthless efficiency that had characterized his conduct of the war the genius of this remarkable man now busied itself with the tasks of peaceful reconstruction. In order to foster the development of industry and trade in Prussia he forbade the import, among other things,[7] of cotton, silk, linen [8] and woollen goods; he sent an expert to England to study tools and methods. In the administration of the state there was nothing which lay outside the field of his personal supervision. He was, he said, "the first servant of the state," but not even [9] the many stories of "Old Fritz" can transform this stiff, stern figure into a benevolent father of his people. He was a despot to the last. "A Prince," he said, "is for society what the head is for the body; he must see, think, act for the whole community." His country became [10] a powerful machine, but when he died the head [11] in both senses had gone, too.

---

1. *sich*. 2. length of time—*die Frist*. 3. *bei*. 4. Tr. "was a European power of the first rank." 5. *zwar*. 6. *immerhin*. 7. *unter anderem*. 8. These can be regarded as nouns forming a multiple compound with "goods," in which case they will be written with capital letters and joined by ＝, the *und* occurring

in the same place as "and." A simpler method is to tr. "goods
of cotton etc." 9. not even—*auch nicht*. 10. *zu* is needed. 11.
Use *Haupt* here.

57. THE FLOOD

They say fear of [1] the unknown can drive a man mad.
I don't know about that. But I did once experience a
danger that was only too obvious and before the night
was over [2] I was on my knees praying and weeping continuously. I am no coward, but to sit there and hear [3]
death coming [4] literally up the stairs is no joke, believe
me. It was the night [5] the dam broke. A million tons of
water swept down the valley and twenty people and
heaven [6] knows how many cattle and sheep were
drowned in the flood before they could escape. The
ones like me who were lucky were already in bed.
Suddenly I became aware of a rushing and rumbling as
though an aeroplane were coming in through [7] the
window. The walls of the house trembled and I was
out of bed and on the landing in a twinkling. Before I
could go any further I saw the door crash inwards and a
mass of grey water poured in so quickly that the chairs
were bumping against the ceiling before the lights went
out. There was nothing to be done. I got dressed and
then undressed again so as to be able to swim better.
But where to? In this second Flood there could be no
dry land. So I sat on the bed in the darkness and
thought of my past life. At [8] dawn the water reached
the first floor but rose no higher. I was out of danger,
but it was a fearful night.

1. Gen. or *vor*. 2. *vorüber*, *vorbei*. 3. Def. Art. required.
4. use Infin. construction. 5. insert "when." 6. Tr. *Gott*.
7. *zum . . . herein*. 8. *bei*.

58. IN THE MUNICIPAL THEATRE

It was on a Sunday afternoon shortly after the end of the war but there was hardly a seat in the whole theatre which was not taken. The audience was prepared to overlook any [1] shortcomings in the performance, for the three short pieces were to be acted by children from the girls' grammar school and the boys' grammar school. The assembly hall in both schools had been destroyed in air-raids and neither [2] of the two possessed a hall suitable for such an occasion. The two schools had therefore jointly hired the municipal theatre. That was only possible on a Sunday and, despite a certain opposition, the plan had been carried out. First came the speeches and the prize-giving at which [3] all the parents clapped their hands sore, for one could not unknowingly offend one's neighbour by [4] according one child more applause than another. Everyone strove to conceal their [5] boredom and was heartily glad when it was over. Then there was an interval while the stage was cleared and arranged for the presentation of two short comedies by Goethe and an extract from his *Faust*. First the girls performed *A Lover's Caprice*, and in this light-hearted, sentimental piece they were all very charming and delightful. Then the boys had an opportunity to stamp, shout, and push each other about when they performed *The Bourgeois General*. Finally, there came the extract from *Faust*,[6] the Student scene, written when University [7] life in Leipzig was still fresh in the young poet's memory. This scene appears in the original version of the play which was written before Weimar and which was lost for almost a hundred years. Mephistopheles, disguised as Faust, exploits the fame and reputation of the learned Doctor first to bewilder and then to corrupt the inexperienced freshman.

1. *irgendwelche*. 2. *keine*. 3. *wobei*. 4. *dadurch dass*. 5. *i.e.*, "his." 6. insert *und zwar*. 7. Tr. "student life."

59. THE GREAT ELECTOR

It was fortunate for the fate of Prussia that three of the four Hohenzollerns [1] in the hundred and fifty years after the end of the Thirty Years War were exceptionally gifted men. By [2] an ironic chance it was the second, the vain and extravagant Frederick I, who exchanged the name Elector for the title of King, for he has no other claim to fame. Frederick William, the great-grandfather of Frederick the Great, was so successful in the restoration of his country after 1648 that he has always been called the Great Elector. A man of great will-power and energy, he is regarded as the founder of the Prussian civil service and the army, and as the creator of the so-called Prussian spirit. One of his measures, which was at the same time benevolent and useful to his country, arose from his desire to help those being persecuted on religious grounds. After the first stern measures against the Protestants in France, his ambassador in Paris received orders [3] to invite the refugees to emigrate to Brandenburg. Already in 1661 several families came to Berlin to settle there and as their number grew the Elector permitted them to build a church in which the first French service was held in the year 1672. This first community, the cradle of the French colony, consisted of about a hundred families. After the Revocation of the Edict of Nantes, the Elector announced that there was [4] a refuge in Brandenburg for all who wished to come. This wise policy bore rich fruit,[5] for Brandenburg thereby [6] won about 25,000 fresh citizens who in [7] almost every field [8] exercised a favourable influence on the development of the country.

1. No "s." 2. *durch*. 3. Sing. 4. Mood? 5. *Obst* cannot be used in this sense. 6. *dadurch*. 7. *auf*. 8. *Gebiet*.

60. THE LOVER OF ANIMALS

Many years ago I made the acquaintance of an old man who had had a most adventurous life. As a [1] boy he had always been interested in animals and he had a lot of them which he fed and protected. His parents only smiled when [2] they saw him with squirrels, rabbits, and even a [3] tame magpie or a [3] hawk, but when [2] he began to take toads and adders up into his bedroom they objected. When he grew up he became a [1] veterinary surgeon and so great was his knowledge of animals that he soon became famous. In order to study animals not to be found [4] in England he went to countries in Africa, South America and Asia. There he collected all kinds of wild animals. The living he sold to [5] zoos and the dead ones were stuffed and exhibited in museums. At home, where he seldom lived, he had a wonderful collection of souvenirs of [6] his various journeys and he could tell strange stories about them. He was a modest man, who never boasted and one had to know him well before he would [7] talk about himself at all.[8] He was proud of one thing, however,[9] that he never let an animal suffer unnecessarily. Although he sold animals to zoos he hated [10] to see them in captivity and he never went to a circus. Not because the animals were ill treated, on the contrary, but [11] because he did not like to watch while animals were doing tricks which were unnatural for them.

1. omit "a." 2. *als* or *wenn?* 3. Watch case here. 4. make a rel. clause of this. 5. *an.* 6. *an.* 7. *wollte.* 8. *überhaupt.* 9. Insert "*nämlich.*" 10. insert *es.* 11. *aber* or *sondern?*

"A" LEVEL PROSES 1947-52

(Set by The Oxford and Cambridge Schools Examination Board)

61. 1947

For nine days Catherine heard nothing, but on the tenth morning, when she entered the breakfast room Henry held out a letter for her. She thanked him as heartily as though he had written it himself. "It is only from James, however," she said, as she looked at the address. She opened it; it was from Oxford . . . Catherine had not read three lines before her sudden change of expression showed her to be receiving unpleasant news; and Henry, watching her through the whole letter, saw plainly that it ended no better than it began. He was prevented, however, by his father's entrance from making any remark. They sat down to breakfast directly, but Catherine could not eat anything. The letter was continually in her hand, or in her lap, and she looked as if she did not know what she was doing. The General, occupied with his coffee and his newspaper, had luckily no leisure to notice her; to the other two, however, her distress was very visible.

JANE AUSTEN (Adapted)

62. 1948

My master left as soon as he was ready, commending Catherine to my particular care in his absence with orders that she must not wander out of the park, even if I accompanied her. He was away three weeks. The first day or two the girl sat in the corner of the library, too sad for either reading or playing. In that quiet

state she caused me little trouble, but it was succeeded
by a period of impatience and weariness. Since I was
too busy and too old to run about with her, I used to
send her into the park, now on foot and now on a pony
and afterwards listened to her accounts of her real or her
imaginary adventures. I did not fear that she would go
too far away, because the gates were locked, and I
thought she would scarcely venture forth alone even if
they stood wide open. Unluckily I was entirely wrong.
Catherine came to me one morning and said she was
that day an Arabian merchant, going to cross the desert,
and that I must give her enough food for herself and her
beasts.

EMILY BRONTË (Adapted)

63. 1949

Then Phineas had a wonderful piece of luck. There
lived in the town of Galway an eccentric old lady, one
Miss Persse, who was the aunt of Mrs Finn, the mother of
our hero. With this lady old Dr Finn had quarrelled
persistently since his marriage, because she wanted to
interfere in the affairs of his family. And now she died,
leaving three thousand pounds to her nephew. "She
couldn't have done better," said the old gentleman;
"she knew you wanted to be a lawyer. That costs
money, and with this help you can start studying at
once." And Phineas did, in fact, show some industry.
He shut himself up in a room at the back of the house,
and his sisters were told that for four hours each day not
a sound was to be allowed to disturb him. But there were
novels in the room as well as law-books—and it is also
quite possible that he dozed a little now and then.
When Phineas received the legacy, he at once offered to

give his father back all the money he had had from him while in London; but this the Doctor refused. "I have quite enough," he said, "and I don't intend to stop working: the later in life a man works, the more likely he is to live."

ANTHONY TROLLOPE

64. 1950

One winter evening, early in the year 1780, a keen north wind arose as it grew dark. Signboards came crashing on the pavement; chimneys reeled; and many a steeple seemed about to fall. In coffee-houses of the better sort, guests crowded around the fire, forgot to talk politics, and told each other with a secret gladness that the wind grew fiercer every minute. Each humble tavern by the river-side had its group of sailors around the hearth, who related many a dismal tale of shipwreck, hoped that some they knew were safe, and shook their heads in doubt. In private houses, children were listening with timid pleasure to tales of ghosts, of tall figures in white standing by bedsides, and people who had gone to sleep in old churches unnoticed, and had then woken up at dead of night to find themselves alone—or not alone. From time to time someone lifted a finger and cried "Listen!" and then, above the rumbling in the chimney and the patter on the glass, was heard a rushing sound, which shook the walls as though a giant's hand were on them; and then, with a lengthened howl, the waves of wind swept on, and left a moment's interval of rest.

CHARLES DICKENS (Adapted)

65. 1951

The sun is high, the cuckoo is shouting over the valley, and the woods are calling to unknown adventures. . . . Chum knows that I am in a good mood. I think he feels that, in spite of my work, at any moment I may speak the magic word "Walk." What a word that is. No sleep so sound that it will not penetrate its depths and bring him to his feet. He would sacrifice the whole dictionary for that one electric word. That and its brother "Bones." Give him these good, sound, sensible words, and he will gladly forgo all the fancies of the poets and all the rhetoric of the statesmen. . . . Yes, Chum knows very well that I am thinking about him and thinking about him in an uncommonly kindly way. That is the secret of the strange friendship between us. We may love other animals and other animals may return our affection. But the dog is the only animal who has an intelligence that may be compared with ours. Stroke a cat or a horse, and it will have a certain bodily pleasure, but go to Chum and call him "Good dog!" and he experiences a spiritual pleasure. He is pleased because you are pleased.

A. G. Gardiner (Adapted)

66. 1952

Soon I heard the noise of chains. The door was cautiously opened, then shut again as soon as I had passed. "Go into the kitchen and touch nothing," said a voice. I went in, and found myself by firelight in the barest room I had ever seen. On the table were a bowl of porridge, a spoon, and a small jug. The man came towards me. He was a small, narrow-shouldered, pale-faced person; he was unshaven, and his age might have been anything between fifty and seventy. It seemed as though he would not look straight at me. I thought he might perhaps be a servant left behind to watch over that great empty house. "Are you hungry?" he asked. "You can eat that porridge if you like." I said I feared it was his own supper. "Oh," he said, "I can very well do without it." Then suddenly he stretched out his hand and cried, "Let's see the letter." I told him it was intended for Mr Balfour, not him. "And who do you think I am, then?" said he, "Give me Alexander's letter at once!" "How do you come to know my father's name?" "It would be strange if I didn't," he returned. "For he was my younger brother, and little as you seem to like either my face or my house, I'm your uncle all the same, Davie, and you're my nephew."

R. L. STEVENSON (Adapted)

ENGLISH—GERMAN VOCABULARY

1. VILLAGE HOLIDAY

brothers and sisters, die Geschwister
week-end, das Wochenende
usual, gewöhnlich
rent, die Miete
moderate, mässig
be worth it, sich lohnen
health, die Gesundheit
boring, langweilig
spend (time), verbringen

place, der Ort
different, anders
circumstance, der Umstand
delight, entzücken
at second hand, aus zweiter Hand
draw (water), schöpfen
well, der Brunnen
bucket, der Eimer

2. A CONVERSATION

sight, die Sehenswürdigkeit
unfortunately, leider
opportunity, die Gelegenheit
post, die Stellung
hospital, das Krankenhaus
nurse, die Krankenschwester
chiefly, hauptsächlich
improve, verbessern
foreigner, der Ausländer
enterprising, unternehmend, unternehmungslustig
cheeky, frech
talkative, gesprächig

impression, der Eindruck
traffic, der Verkehr
Underground, die Untergrundbahn
invention, die Erfindung
homesick, Heimweh haben
kind, freundlich
take trouble, sich Mühe geben
hostess, die Gastgeberin
take leave, sich verabschieden
avoid, vermeiden
crush, das Gedränge

3. THE OLD FARMER

comfortable, bequem
armchair, der Sessel
lawn, der Rasen
sheep dog, der Schäferhund
grandchild, der Enkel
fishing rod, die Angelrute
trout, die Forelle
catch, fangen

be careful, sich in acht nehmen, vorsichtig sein, acht haben
polite, höflich
generous, freigebig
go on, continue (intr.), fortfahren
in any case, jedenfalls
dangerous, gefährlich

worry, sich Sorgen machen, Angst haben
set off, sich auf den Weg machen
bark, bellen
tail, der Schwanz

wag, wedeln (mit)
fence, der Zaun
consider, halten (für)
superfluous, überflüssig
unfold, entfalten

4. AT THE ZOO

zoo, der Zoo (logischer Garten), der Tiergarten
cage, der Käfig
carnivore, das Raubtier
feeding time, die Fütterung ⎫
feed, füttern ⎬ of animals
food, das Futter ⎭
monkey. der Affe
monkey-nut, die Erdnuss, ··e
bar of cage, das Gitter, der Stab
paw, die Tatze, die Pfote
claw, die Kralle
seize, ergreifen
yawn, gähnen
stretch, sich recken
doze, schlummern, dösen
impatiently, ungeduldig

roar, brüllen
thrust, stossen
huge, gewaltig
tear to pieces, zerreissen
devour, verschlingen, a, u; auffressen
creature, das Geschöpf
sea lion, der Seelöwe
seal, die Robbe, der Seehund
dive, tauchen
give away, verschenken
supply, der Vorrat
trunk, der Rüssel
skilful, geschickt
exit, der Ausgang
ostrich, der Strauss
hippopotamus, das Nilpferd
specially, besonders

5. THE BAY

step, der Schritt
spot, die Stelle
cliff, die Klippe
top to bottom, oben bis unten
at least, wenigstens
steep, steil
rugged, schroff
slope, der Abhang
seagull, die Möwe
circle, kreisen
glide, segeln, gleiten
to and fro, hin und her
seaweed, der Seetang
brightly coloured, bunt

cave, die Höhle
pirate, der Seeräuber
capture, gefangennehmen
surf, die Brandung
leave behind, liegenlassen
suggest, vorschlagen
crab, der Krebs
climb, hinaufklettern
allow, erlauben (with Dat.)
hurry, sich beeilen
tide (incoming), die Flut
bay, die Bucht
lifeboat, das Rettungsboot
rescue, bergen, retten

6. THE HILL

reach, erreichen
summit, der Gipfel
hill, der Hügel
breathless, atemlos
panting, keuchend
strenuous, anstrengend
climb, der Aufstieg
refreshing, erfrischend
breeze, leichter Wind
drink, das Getränk
stir, bewegen
match, das Streichholz, ·· er
cigarette, die Zigarette
light, anzünden
stretch, extend, sich erstrecken
plain, die Ebene
map, die Landkarte
shine, schimmern
ribbon, das Band, ·· er
wind (along), sich (hin)
  schlängeln
hedge, die Hecke
divide, trennen
cattle, das Vieh
refuge, die Zuflucht

cornfield, das Getreidefeld
shade (of colour), die Abstu-
  fung
distance, die Entfernung
wheat, der Weizen
barley, die Gerste
oats, der Hafer
identify, erkennen
hay, das Heu
harvest, die Ernte
haystack, der Heuschober
patch, der Fleck
ploughland, das Ackerland
stretch, die Strecke
presumably, vermutlich
root crops, die Rüben
cabbage, der Kohl
activity, die Tätigkeit
object, der Gegenstand
toy, das Spielzeug
hover, schweben
hawk, der Habicht
lark, die Lerche
hop, hüpfen
hawthorn, der Hagedorn

7. WEINSBERG

beginning, der Anfang
century, das Jahrhundert
besiege, belagern
outcome, der Ausgang
quote, zitieren
feminine, weiblich
courage, die Tapferkeit
faithfulness, die Treue
garrison, die Besatzung
surround, umgeben (insep.),
  einschliessen
stronghold, die Festung
swear (an oath), schwören, u, o
show mercy to, begnadigen

assert, beteuern
innocence, die Unschuld
depart, abziehen
unharmed, unversehrt
possession(s), der Besitz, das
  Besitztum
strange, sonderbar
procession, der Zug
totter, wanken
trick, betrügen, o, o
strike down, erschlagen
allow, permit, erlauben
keep (word), halten
save, retten

8. ON THE CHURCH TOWER

church tower, der Kirchturm
view, die Aussicht
map, die Karte (Landkarte)
hill, der Hügel
in the distance, in der Ferne
name, nennen
spend (time), verbringen
occur to, einfallen (*with Dat.*)
spiral staircase, die Wendeltreppe
locked, verschlossen
suggest, vorschlagen
divide, separate, trennen
churchyard, der Kirchhof
try, versuchen
consider, think, nachdenken
bell, die Glocke

lead, führen
place, die Stelle
ring, läuten
catch sight of, erblicken
broom, der Besen
leaning, angelehnt
handle, der Stiel
attempt, der Versuch
catch, deal (a blow), versetzen
blow, der Schlag
hefty, kräftig
deafening, betäubend
die away (of sound), verklingen, a, u
deaf, taub
Vicar, der Pfarrer

9. ARRIVAL

that is, das heisst
policeman, der Polizist
ask a question, eine Frage stellen
correct, verbessern
mistake, der Fehler
different, anders
address, ansprechen
real, genuine, echt
reply, die Antwort
unexpected, unerwartet
accent, die Aussprache
probably, wahrscheinlich
grow accustomed, sich gewöhnen an (*with Acc.*)
thank goodness, Gott sei Dank
all the same, immerhin
meet, fetch, abholen

hardly, kaum
expect, erwarten
arrange, verabreden
decent, anständig
laugh at, auslachen
verb, das Zeitwort, das Verbum
sentence, der Satz
wrong, falsch
look like, ähneln, ähnlich sehen (*with Dat.*)
ride (a bicycle), radeln, Rad fahren
hold out, reichen
try, versuchen
teach, lehren
suitcase, der Handkoffer
flat, die Wohnung
grand, grossartig

10. PRISONER OF WAR

prisoner of war, der Kriegsgefangene
difficulty, die Schwierigkeit
quarry, der Steinbruch
bullet, die Kugel
hit, treffen, i, a, o
draw, ziehen
pistol, die Pistole
seize, fassen
wait for, expect, erwarten
battle, die Schlacht
fierce, grimmig
kill, töten
disarm, entwaffnen
lift up, aufheben
guess, vermuten, erraten

headquarters, das Hauptquartier
memorize, sich merken
direction, die Richtung
pain, der Schmerz
severe, acute, heftig
consciousness, das Bewusstsein
bare, kahl
wound, die Wunde
bind up, verbinden, a, u
rough, coarse, grob
blanket, die Wolldecke
news die Nachricht
acquaintance, der Bekannte
stoop, sich bücken
Captain, Hauptmann

11. COUSIN FROM CANADA

cousin, der Vetter, n
distance, die Entfernung
imagine, sich denken. vorstellen
countryside, die Landschaft
ugly, hässlich
resemble, gleichen, i, i (*with Dat.*)
box, die Kiste
brick, der Ziegel
wretched, elend
hen, das Huhn, ¨er
scratch, kratzen
nettle, die Nessel
weed(s), das Unkraut
neglect, vernachlässigen
unseen, invisible. unsichtbar
furtive, verstohlen
arrival, die Ankunft
movement, die Bewegung

chimney, der Schornstein
rise, steigen
washing, die Wäsche
line, die Leine
impression, der Eindruck
stay, der Aufenthalt
stupid, dumm
knock, klopfen
door bell, die Klingel
step, der Tritt, der Schritt
hall, die Diele
key, der Schlüssel
groan, stöhnen
lock, das Schloss, ¨er
bolt, der Riegel
suspiciously, argwöhnisch
crack, die Spalte
add, hinzufügen
straight, direkt
gaol, das Zuchthaus

12. SHIPWRECK

shipwreck, der Schiffbruch
suggest, vorschlagen
wet, rainy, regnerisch
schoolroom, das Schulzimmer
doll, die Puppe
be bored, sich langweilen
survivor, der Überlebende
island, die Insel, n
Pacific, der Stille Ozean
collect, sammeln
thing, object, der Gegenstand, ¨e
be wrecked, scheitern
axe, die Axt, ¨e
saw, die Säge
gun, das Gewehr
box, die Schachtel
match, das Streichholz, ¨er
magnifying glass, das Vergrösserungsglas
mean, meinen
light (fire), anzünden
food, die Nahrungsmittel (*pl.*)
note-book, das Heft, e
describe, beschreiben
adventure, das Abenteuer
be drowned, ertrinken, a, u
struggle, kämpfen
wave, die Welle
have a rest, sich ausruhen
dry, trocken
leaf, das Blatt, ¨er
lie down, sich hinlegen

cushion, das Kissen
groan, stöhnen
be no use, keinen Zweck haben
chocolate, die Schokolade
count, be reckoned, gelten, i, a, o
real, genuine, echt
edible, essbar
although, obgleich, obschon
dirty, schmutzig
build, bauen
nightfall, der Sonnenuntergang
in case, falls
savage, der Wilde (*Adj. as Noun*)
snake, die Schlange
object, protest, einwenden, a, a
monkey, der Affe, n
goat, die Ziege
useful, nützlich
at least, wenigstens
remember, sich erinnern (an *with Acc.*)
throw, werfen, i, a, o
coconut, die Kokosnuss, ¨e
save, rescue, retten
thirst, der Durst
spring, die Quelle
hole, das Loch, ¨er
shell, die Schale
liquid, die Flüssigkeit
turtle, die Schildkröte
hard-boiled, hartgekocht

13. THE ENVY OF THE GODS

envy, der Neid
the Gods, die Götter
tyrant, der Tyrann, en, en
palace, der Palast
look, schauen
island, die Insel

rule, beherrschen
Egypt, Ägypten
fortunate, glücklich
fortune, das Glück
kind, favourable, günstig
your equals, deinesgleichen

subject, der Untertan, en
arrival, die Ankunft
messenger, der Bote, n, n
gift, das Geschenk
rival, der Gegner
danger, die Gefahr, en
threaten, drohen
fleet, die Flotte
be wrecked, scheitern
Cretan, kretisch, der Kreter (*of the Cretans*)
army, das Heer, die Armee
approach, sich nähern (*with Dat.*)
shore, der Strand
hardly, kaum
laden, beladen
booty, die Beute
come to anchor, vor Anker gehen

harbour, der Hafen
sailor, der Matrose, n
report, berichten
jubilation, der Jubel
destroy, vernichten
beware of, sich hüten vor
propitiate, versöhnen
sacrifice, opfern
possession, der Besitz
lord, master, der Gebieter
present, schenken
catch, fangen
cut up, zerteilen
costly, kostbar
stomach, der Magen
hasten, eilen
bound(ary), die Grenze
take ship, sich einschiffen
dash to pieces, zerschmettern

14. BELSHAZZAR

Belshazzar, Belsazar
midnight, die Mitternacht
ancient, uralt
sunk, versunken
sleep, der Schlaf
palace, der Palast
feast, schmausen
retinue, das Gefolge
wild, wild
abandon, die Ausgelassenheit
flicker, flackern
torch, die Fackel
flow, fliessen, o, o
glow, glühen
pride, der Stolz
unnoticed, unbemerkt
secret, heimlich
order, der Befehl
servant, der Diener
disappear, verschwinden, a, u
banquet hall, der Festsaal

gold (*Adj.*), golden
silver (*Adj.*), silbern
vessel, das Gefäss, e
temple, der Tempel
seize, ergreifen, i, i
goblet, der Becher
fill, füllen
brim, der Rand, ··er
empty, leeren
draught, der Zug
blasphemy, die Lästerung
hurl, schleudern
scorn, der Hohn
defiance, der Trotz
finally, schliesslich
crazy, toll
arrogance, der Übermut
laughter, das Gelächter
fall silent, verstummen
tremble, zittern
limb, das Glied, er

fear, die Furcht
dread, das Grauen
monstrous gigantic, riesenhaft
trace, draw, zeichnen
letter, der Buchstabe, n, n
whitewashed, getüncht
wall (interior), die Wand, ⸚e
pale, bleich
send for, holen lassen.
magi, die Magier (*pl.*)
interpret, deuten
writing, die Schrift
clothe, kleiden

purple, der Purpur
chain, die Kette
neck, der Hals
dumb, stumm
keep, behalten
gift, die Gabe
number, count, zählen
kingdom, das Königreich
finish, vollenden
weigh, wiegen, o, o
balance(s), die Wage or Waage
divide, zerteilen
slay, kill, töten

15. MRS BRANDT GOES SHOPPING

do shopping, Einkäufe machen
put on, aufsetzen
in itself, an sich
difficult, schwierig
undertaking, die Unternehmung
send, schicken
baker, der Bäcker, die Bäckerei
smile at, anlächeln
literally, buchstäblich
child's play, das Kinderspiel
housewife, die Hausfrau
housekeeping, der Haushalt
responsible, verantwortlich
mistake, der Fehler
shake, schütteln
free, los
childish, kindisch
thought, der Gedanke, n
make sure, sich versichern
purse, der Geldbeutel
door key, der Hausschlüssel
handbag, die (Hand) tasche
basket, der Korb
bus, der Autobus
stop, die Haltestelle

post office, das Postamt
stamp, die Briefmarke
besides, ausserdem
clerk, der Angestellte (*Adj. as Noun*)
counter, der Schalter
acquaintance, der Bekannte (*Adj. as Noun*)
beat, klopfen
butcher, der Fleischer, die Fleischerei
beef, das Rindfleisch
mutton, das Hammelfleisch
pork, das Schweinefleisch
veal, das Kalbfleisch
distinguish, unterscheiden
husband, der Mann
expensive, teuer, kostbar
polite, höflich
tradesman, der Verkäufer
shop, der Laden, ⸚
certainly, gewiss
victory, der Sieg
Army commander, der Feldherr
tired, müde

16. AUTUMN IN THE MOUNTAINS

wooden, hölzern
bridge, die Brücke
leather (*Adj.*), ledern
strap, der Riemen
dangle, baumeln
tinkle, schellen
ring, klingeln
note, der Ton
size, die Grösse
soft, sanft
gentle, mild
dainty, zierlich
creature, das Geschöpf, e
enormous, sehr gross
stroll, schlendern
leather trousers (**shorts**), die Lederhosen
stocking, der Strumpf, ¨e
switch (**stick**), die Gerte
cut the head off, köpfen
thistle, die Distel
moment, der Augenblick
watch, nachsehen (*with Dat.*)
stream, brook, der Bach, ¨e

need, brauchen, nötig haben
meadow, die Wiese
as soon as, sobald
peak, der Gipfel, die Spitze
valley, das Tal, ¨er
summit, die Spitze, der Gipfel
bathed, gebadet
fiery, feurig
ray, der Strahl, en
height, die Höhe
melt, schmelzen, i, o, o
place, die Stelle
precipice, der Abgrund, ¨e
steep, steil
edge, der Rand
glacier, der Gletscher
cross, überschreiten, i, i (*insep.*)
highest, höchstgelegen
mountaineer, der Bergsteiger
winter sports enthusiast, der Wintersportfreund
expect, erwarten
shut in, einsperren

17. MISS SCRATTON

previous, vorig, vergangen
member, das Mitglied, der Angehörige (*Adj. as Noun*)
neglect, vernachlässigen
purposely, absichtlich, mit Absicht
busy, beschäftigt
affairs, die Angelegenheiten
funeral, die Beerdigung, das Begräbnis
married, verheiratet
pay (**a visit**), abstatten
kindness, die Freundlichkeit

be in the way, einem im Wege sein
spend (**time**), verleben, verbringen
perceive, erkennen
meaning, die Bedeutung
in fact, tatsächlich, in der Tat
inherit, erben
considerable, beträchtlich
reward, die Belohnung
wasted, verloren
add, hinzufügen
hasty, hastig

task, die Aufgabe
marry (get married), sich
  verheiraten
emigrate, auswandern
contain, enthalten
invitation, die Einladung

estate, das Gut
hesitate, zögern
accept, annehmen
travel bureau, das Reisebüro
inquire, sich erkundigen (über
  with Acc.)

18. MARTIN LUTHER

fling, schleudern
inkwell, das Tintenfass
mark, der Fleck
ink spot, der Klecks
humble, niedrig
origin, die Herkunft
content, zufrieden
lawyer, der Rechtsanwalt
monastery, das Kloster
monk, der Mönch
Pope, der Papst
horror, das Entsetzen
fill, erfüllen

writings, die Schriften
opinion, die Meinung
heretical, ketzerisch
sermon, die Predigt
danger of life, Lebensgefahr
hide, verbergen, verstecken
translation, die Übersetzung
  (ins with Acc.)
passionate, leidenschaftlich
mind, der Geist, das Gemüt
doubt, der Zweifel
influential, einflussreich

19. IN AN ART GALLERY

art gallery, die Gemäldegalerie
be bored (to death), sich (zu
  Tode) langweilen
art, die Kunst
refuse, sich weigern
mackintosh, der Regenmantel
take refuge, (sich) flüchten
entrance, der Eingang
disagreeable, unangenehm
surprise, die Überraschung
admission fee, das Eintritts-
  geld
yawn, gähnen
stream, strömen
window-pane, die Fenster-
  scheibe
bright, hell
escape, entfliehen, o, o

mostly, meistens, zum grössten
  Teil
drawing, die (Hand) zeichnung
engraving, der Kupferstich, e
water-colour, das Aquarell, e
(oil) painting, das (Öl) gemälde
bright, bunt
careful, sorgfältig
sailing, das Segeln
speciality, das Fach
grin, das Grinsen
youthful, jugendlich
interest, interessieren
funny, komisch
set, setzen
sail, das Segel
sink (Intr.), (ver) sinken, a, u
paint, malen

20. THE WEATHER

dining-room, der Speisesaal
tap, leicht klopfen
barometer, das/der Barometer
usual, gewohnt, üblich
address, anreden
periodical, die Zeitschrift
lower, senken
disclose, enthüllen
amiable, gutmütig, liebenswürdig
feature, der Gesichtszug, ·ˑe
Bishop, der Bischof
willing, bereit
topic, das Thema
pursue, verfolgen
drought, die Trockenheit, die Durre
agree with, übereinstimmen mit
continue, fortfahren (*Intr.*)
varied, mannigfaltig
in regard to, in Bezug auf (*with Acc.*)
express, äussern

satisfy, (*Dat.*) Genüge tun
townsfolk, Stadtleute
hardly, kaum
take into account, in Betracht ziehen
form, bilden
background, der Hintergrund
grumble, murren (über)
cheer, aufmuntern
influence, der Einfluss
carry out, ausführen
sailor, der Matrose, n
pilot, der Flieger
professional sportsman, der Berufssportler
interrupt, unterbrechen
exaggerate, übertreiben
indifference, die Gleichgültigkeit
town dweller, der Städter
respect, die Hinsicht
occupation, der Beruf
agree, einig sein

21. THE OLD FLOWER-SELLER

basket, der Korb, ·ˑe
spot, der Fleck, die Stelle
step, die Stufe
fountain, der Brunnen, Laufbrunnen
museum, das Museum, Museen
coloured, bunt
umbrella, der Regenschirm
belong, gehören
square, der Platz, ·ˑe
cheerful, munter
as a rule, in der Regel
cheap, billig
smile, das Lächeln

business man, der Geschäftsmann, -leute
office, das Büro, s
properly, richtig
carnation, die Nelke
buttonhole, das Knopfloch
bunch, das Sträusschen, der Strauss
heather, das Heidekraut
treat, behandeln
respect, die Achtung Ehrfurcht
nod, nicken
arrest, verhaften
violet, das Veilchen

fasten, befestigen
pin, die Stecknadel
pretty, hübsch
artist, der Künstler
portrait, das Bildnis

famous, berühmt
refuse, sich weigern
studio, das Atelier
paint, malen

22. AN INTERRUPTED MEAL

meal, die Mahlzeit
interrupt, unterbrechen
bean, die Bohne
cauliflower, der Blumenkohl
prefer, vorziehen, lieber haben
help oneself, sich bedienen
answer, antworten
envy, beneiden
vegetable(s), das Gemüse
taste, schmecken
really, wirklich
fresh, frisch
often, manchmal, oft
regret, bedauern
grow (Tr.), anbauen
wonder, sich fragen
be worth while, sich lohnen
strawberry, die Erdbeere
pea, die Erbse
pick, pflücken
favourable, günstig
dry, trocken
brussels sprouts, der Rosen-
kohl
tomato, die Tomate
ripen, reifen, reif werden
thankful, dankbar

farmer, der Bauer
hand, reichen
bowl, die Schüssel
raspberry, die Himbeere
conversation, das Gespräch
ring, klingeln
telephone, das Telephon
excuse, entschuldigen
moment, der Augenblick
return, zurückkehren
I am sorry, es tut mir leid
mine, das Bergwerk
at once, sofort
accident, das Unglück
serious, bad, schlimm
hurt, verletzt
workman, der Arbeiter
shaft, der Schacht, ¨e
rescue squad, die Rettungs-
mannschaft
suspect, ahnen
control oneself, sich beherrschen
express, zum Ausdruck bringen
anxiety, die Angst
be careful, sich in acht nehmen

23. THE TRAVELLING JOURNEYMAN

travelling, wandering,
fahrend
journeyman, der Geselle, n, n
rise, origin, die Entstehung
trade union, die Gewerkschaft
craftsman, der Handwerker

belong to, angehören (with
Dat.)
guild, die Zunft, ¨e
apprentice, der Lehrling
complete, vollenden
training, die Ausbildung

be the custom, üblich, gebräuchlich sein
at that time, damals
Romantic, der Romantiker
symbol, das Sinnbild, er
longing, nostalgia, die Sehnsucht
stride, schreiten, i, i
gaily, munter
dawn, der Sonnenaufgang
therefore, daher, also
catch sight of, erblicken
clearing, die Lichtung
beg (*Tr.*), erbetteln
steaming, dampfend
plate, der Teller
knock, anklopfen
sign of life, das Lebenszeichen
temptation, die Versuchung
bold, dreist, keck
wipe, wischen
gravy, die Tunke
make oneself comfortable, es sich bequem machen
stove, der Ofen, Öfen

awake (*Intr.*), erwachen, aufwachen
stir, move about, sich rühren
go for a stroll, einen Gang machen
living room, das Wohnzimmer
laid, gedeckt
ready, vorbereitet
supper, das Abendbrot
fellow, der Bursch, Kerl
intimidate, einschüchtern
fall to, zugreifen, i, i
for the moment, vorläufig
gradually, allmählich
creep, move, rücken
gloom, darkness, die Dunkelheit
start, jump, zusammenzucken
stand, endure, ertragen
bewitched, verhext
path, der Pfad
shine, leuchten
empty, leer
cry, der Schrei
horror, das Entsetzen
sight, die Sicht

24. THE GARDENER

gardener, der Gärtner
friendship, die Freundschaft
last, dauern
divide, einteilen
part, der Teil, e
interval, der Zwischenraum
patient, geduldig
call (**angrily**), schelten, i, a, o
naughty, unartig
spoil, verderben, i, a, o
touch, berühren
drive, treiben, ie, ie; jagen
dig, graben, ä, u, a
plant, pflanzen

wheelbarrow, der Schubkarren
clamber, klettern
pretend, tun als ob
trundle, rollen
rubber, der Gummi
tyre, der Reifen
uncomfortable, unbequem
trip, die Fahrt
prize, schätzen
all the same, immerhin
reward, die Belohnung
privilege, das Vorrecht
set out, aussetzen
vegetable, das Gemüse

sometimes, manchmal
properly, correctly, richtig
be afraid, Angst haben
injure, damage, beschädigen
polite, höflich
devise, ersinnen, a, o
excuse, der Vorwand, ̈e
get rid of, (etwas) loswerden
to rights, straight, in Ordnung
(bringen)
press, drücken
earth, die Erde
hard, firm, fest
thumb, der Daumen
tread, treten, i, a, e
flourish, gedeihen, ie, ie
bright, bunt

secretly, im Stillen
prefer, vorziehen
basket, der Korb, ̈e
pea, die Erbse
massive, gewaltig, mächtig
cauliflower, der Blumenkohl
shine, beam, strahlen
pride, der Stolz
pleasure, die Freude
berry, die Beere
wait for, warten auf (*with Acc.*)
answer, die Antwort
juicy, saftig
delicious, köstlich
spit, spucken
tough, zäh
skin, die Haut, ̈e

25. THE DIARY

duty, die Pflicht
desk, der Schreibtisch
burn (*Tr.*), verbrennen
relatives, die Verwandten
scattered, zerstreut
furniture, die Möbel (*N. pl.*)
auction, versteigern
bear, ertragen
allow, erlauben (*with Dat.*)
volume, der Band, ̈e
author, der Verfasser
bound, eingebunden
in manuscript, mit der Hand
geschrieben
publication, die Veröffentlich-
ung
mention, erwähnen
diary, journal, das Tagebuch
admire, bewundern
leisure, die Musse
position, die Lage
patient, der Patient, en, en
learn, erfahren

friend, der, die Bekannte, n
hide, verbergen
admit, gestehen
incident, der Vorfall, ̈e
without restraint, ungebän-
digt
stage, die Bühne
tragedy, die Tragödie
comedy, die Komödie
example, das Beispiel
selfless, selbstlos
courage, der Mut
sympathy, das Mitgefühl
profession, der Beruf
constantly, beständig
necessary, notwendig
contact, die Berührung
misfortune, das Unglück
surprise, überraschen
role, die Rolle
adviser, der Ratgeber
confessor, der Beichtvater
thrust on, aufdringen (*with Dat.*)

26. AN OLD-FASHIONED SMITH

old-fashioned, altmodisch
choke, ersticken
cloud, die Wolke
smoke, der Rauch
arise, entstehen
hide, hüllen
stooping, gebeugt
figure, die Gestalt
smith, der Schmied
place, legen
glow, glühen
iron, das Eisen
hoof, der Huf, e
leathern, ledern
apron, die Schürze
patient, geduldig
horseshoe, das Hufeisen
fasten, befestigen
by means of, mittels (*with Gen.*)
nail, der Nagel, ¨
straighten one's back, sich aufrichten
trade, das Gewerbe
nowadays, heutzutage
at the most, höchstens
crowd off, verdrängen
last, hold out, aushalten

tractor, der Trekker
do, carry out, verrichten
team of horses, das Gespann
ploughman, der Ackersmann
repair, die Reparatur
garage, die Garage
down yonder, drunten
tyre, der Reifen, –,
point to, weisen auf
plough, der Pflug
chain, die Kette
agricultural, landwirtschaftlich
implements, das Gerät
apprentice, der Geselle, n
important, wichtig
surname, der Familienname
prove, beweisen
shrug shoulders, die Achseln zucken
origin, die Herkunft
strike, occur to, auffallen (*with Dat.*)
fall silent, verstummen
nigh on, beinahe
go out, erlöschen, erlischt, o, o
be sorry, bedauern

27. CONVALESCENCE

convalescence, die Genesung
deck-chair, der Liegestuhl
pine tree, die Kiefer
view, die Aussicht
bay, die Bucht
by nature, von Natur
lazy, faul
illness, die Krankheit
weaken, erschlaffen
content, zufrieden

discover, entdecken
desire, die Lust
rug, die Wolldecke
cover, bedecken
pleasant, angenehm
flower bed, das Beet, e
unknown, unbekannt
please, erfreuen
sound, call, der Ruf
pigeon, die Taube

peaceful, friedlich
accompaniment, die Begleitung
movement, die Bewegung
foliage, das Laub
attract, anziehen
attention, die Aufmerksamkeit
well, healthy, gesund
busy, beschäftigt
just, simply, einfach
squirrel, das Eichhörnchen
that is, das heisst
at all, überhaupt
notice, bemerken
give pleasure, Freude machen (*with Dat.*)
brisk, flink
bushy, buschig
tail, der Schwanz
watch, beobachten
scarcely, kaum
moment, der Augenblick
ant, die Ameise
climb, klettern

procession, der Zug
trunk, der Stamm
weary, ermüden
monotonous, eintönig
industrious, fleissig, emsig
personification, die Verkörperung
virtue, die Tugend
for the moment, augenblicklich, vorläufig
imitate, nachahmen
gradually, allmählich
buzz, summen
insect, das Insekt, en
bee, die Biene
rustle, rauschen
branch, twig, der Zweig
scent, der Duft, ¨e
numb, betäuben
sense, der Sinn, e
awake, wachend
wait for, warten auf
patient, geduldig

28. BIRTHDAY IN LONDON

birthday, der Geburtstag
wake up (*Intr.*), aufwachen
expect, erwarten
stay, der Aufenthalt
bus, der Autobus, usse
taxi, das Taxi, s
wake (*Tr.*), wecken
be ashamed, sich schämen
result, die Folge
exciting, aufregend
exhausting, anstrengend
describe, beschreiben
envy, beneiden
in the first place, erstens
choose, wählen
arrange, prepare, vorbereiten

secret, das Geheimnis
cash, einwechseln
cheque, der Scheck
Daddy, Pappi
as a present, geschenkt
hunt, jagen, auf die Jagd gehen (nach)
have a good look at, gründlich ansehen
bracelet, das Armband
trip, der Ausflug
up river, den Fluss hinauf, stromauf
ice, das Speiseeis
book, bestellen
seat, der Platz, ¨e

opera, die Oper
marriage, die Hochzeit
adore, schwärmen für
performance, die Aufführung
stage, die Bühne
make-up, die Schminke
actor, der Schauspieler

without difficulty, mühelos
it was fun, es machte (mir)
Spass
conductor, der Dirigent, en, en
be thrilled, begeistert sein
look forward to, sich freuen
auf

29. OUT SHOOTING

NOTE: Terms connected with hunting have to be handled with care. *Die Jagd* is no more the exact equivalent of "hunting" than is *la classe;* it is often "shooting" and *auf der Jagd* is the translation for the title of this piece.

impression, der Eindruck, ¨e
awake (Tr.), wecken
thrust, schieben, o, o
ready, bereit, fertig
yawn, gähnen
miserable, unglücklich
get dressed, sich anziehen
warm up (Tr.), erwärmen
experience, das Erlebnis, sse
gradually, allmählich
appear (to one), (einem)
vorkommen
foolish, albern
on the way, unterwegs
otherwise, sonst
waste, verschwenden
detour, der Umweg
scent (Tr.), wittern
elapse, verlaufen
grow light, dämmern
sign, beckon, winken
edge, der Rand, ¨er
track, der Weg, der Pfad
destination, das Ziel
hidden, versteckt
bush, der Busch, ¨e
twitter, zwitschern
now and again, dann und wann

harsh (of sound), gellend
laugh, das Lachen
jay, der Eichelhäher
magpie, die Elster
observe, betrachten
gun, das Gewehr
at the same time, zugleich
shotgun, die Flinte
sporting rifle, die Büchse
barrel (of gun), der Lauf, ¨e
popular, beliebt
deer, das Reh, e
comparatively, verhältnis-
mässig
common, frequent, häufig
so called, sogenannt
triplet, der Drilling
armed, ready for, gerüstet
(für)
game, das Wild
kind, sort, die Art
hare, der Hase, n, n
pheasant, der Fasan, e
partridge, das Rebhuhn, ¨er
small shot, der Schrot
(rifle) bullet, die Kugel
careful, vorsichtig
raise, erheben, o, o

slip, glide, schleichen, i, i
feed (*Intr.*)**,** weiden
unsuspecting, ahnungslos

distance, die Entfernung
take aim, zielen
fire, abdrücken

30. THE STORM

storm, der Sturm, ⏜e, das Unwetter
used to, gewohnt an (*with Acc.*)
out of the ordinary, ausserordentlich
shriek, schreien
howl, heulen
madman, der Irrsinnige (*Adj. as Noun*)
continuously, ununterbrochen
beach, der Strand
background, der Hintergrund
bare, kahl, nackt
branch, der Ast, Äste
farmhouse, das Bauernhaus
sway, schwanken
wild, wild
stream, strömen
scatter, zerstreuen
fortunately, glücklicherweise
stall, der Stall, ⏜e
upright, aufrecht
thrust, die Wucht
catch hold of, fassen

loose, locker
move, bewegen
sweep, fegen
hen-house, das Hühnerhaus, der Hühnerstall
meadow, die Wiese
push, schieben, treiben
direction, die Richtung
change, ändern
topple over, umkippen
rattle, rasseln, klappern
force, die Gewalt
pebble, der Kieselstein
twig, der Zweig
pane, die Scheibe
noise, der Lärm
damage, der Schaden, Schäden
news, die Nachricht(en)
learn, hear, erfahren
tide, die Flut
gigantic, riesenhaft
form, bilden
dyke, der Deich, e
flood (*Tr.*)**,** überschwemmen
seaside town, die Küstenstadt

31. THE VILLAGE SHOP

shop, der Laden, ⏜
entrance, der Eingang, ⏜e
display window, das Schaufenster
sign, das Schild, er
groceries, Kolonialwaren
chemist, die Apotheke
drapers, das Kurzwarengeschäft

contain, enthalten
telephone, das Telephon
owner, Inhaber (in)
manager, Geschäftsführer(in)
saleswoman, die Verkäuferin
elderly, ältlich
cheerful, munter
vigorous, rüstig
née, geborene

care for, sorgen für

unmarried, ledig, unverheiratet

keep house, den Haushalt führen

deliver, liefern

expensive, teuer, wertvoll

excuse, der Vorwand, ''e

need, brauchen, nötig haben

soap powder, das Seifenpulver

picture postcard, die Ansichtskarte

be in a hurry, Eile haben, es eilig haben

gossip, der Klatsch

rumour, das Gerücht, e

in the least, im geringsten, keineswegs

malicious, tückisch

on the contrary, im Gegenteil

help, Hilfe leisten

stormy, stürmisch

telegram, das Telegramm

take amiss, übel nehmen

bad, schlecht

news, die Nachrichten

congratulations, (meine) Glückwünsche

32. THE HERMIT

hermit, der Einsiedler

edge, der Rand, ''er

tumbledown, baufällig

mushroom, der Pilz, e

thatched roof, das Strohdach

whitewashed, getüncht

picturesque, malerisch

gable, der Giebel

crooked, schief

structure, das Gebäude

be missing, fehlen

completely, völlig

attic, der Boden

step, treten, i, a, e

gap, die Lücke

fence, der Zaun, ''e

goat, die Ziege

barn, die Scheune

trot, traben

bleat, meckern

towards, auf (Acc.) . . . zu

indignant, unwillig

dratted, verflucht

let loose, losbinden, a, u

rush out, herausstürzen

seize, ergreifen, i, i

tug, ziehen

drag, schleppen

shed, der Schuppen

disappear, verschwinden, a, u

assert, beteuern

innocence, die Unschuld

angry, zornig

inn, das Wirtshaus

learn, erfahren, ä, u, a

encounter, begegnen (with Dat.)

son-in-law, der Schwiegersohn

refuse, sich weigern

endure, erdulden

miserable, elend

conditions, die Verhältnisse (N. pl.)

condition, state, der Zustand, ''e

well, der Brunnen

drop, der Tropfen

determined, fest entschlossen

consider, halten für

mad, verrückt

33. THE MESSENGER

messenger, der Bote
rein, der Zügel
force to a halt, zum Stehen bringen
foam-flecked, schaumbefleckt
swear, fluchen
believe, glauben (*with Dat.*)
blow (up), sprengen (*Tr.*)
current, die Strömung
make a decision, sich entscheiden, einen Entschluss fassen
mouth (of river), die Mündung
destroy, zerstören
upstream, stromauf
enemy, der Feind
situation, die Lage
victory, der Sieg
defeat, die Niederlage
depend on, abhängen von
news, die Botschaft, die Nachricht
spur, der Sporn, Sporen
belly, der Bauch
gallop, galoppieren
ferry, die Fähre
overlook, übersehen (*insep.*)

hurried, hastig
retreat, der Rückzug
lessen, vermindern
speed, die Geschwindigkeit
gap, die Lücke
hedge, die Hecke
meadow, die Wiese
avoid, vermeiden
detour, der Umweg
sunken road, der Hohlweg
dismount, absteigen
untie, losbinden, a, u
row, rudern
neigh, wiehern
plunge, sich stürzen
back, der Rücken
strength, die Kraft
quiver, zittern
steam, der Dampf
rise, steigen, ie, ie
pant, keuchen
body, der Leib, er; der Körper
thrust, der Stoss, ¨e
plank, die Planke
exhausted, erschöpft
overcome, überwinden, a, u; überstehen
goal, das Ziel

34. SPRING IN THE COUNTRY

walking-stick, der Spazierstock
chapter, das Kapitel
distract, ablenken
hedge, die Hecke
thicket, das Dickicht
orchard, der Obstgarten
thrush, die Drossel
blackbird, die Amsel
branch, der Ast, ¨e

neighbouring, benachbart
cuckoo, der Kuckuck
monotonous, eintönig
blossom, die Blüte
plum, die Pflaume
pear, die Birne
wallflower, der Goldlack (*no plural*)
tulip, die Tulpe
despise, verachten

dandelion, der Löwenzahn
patch, der Fleck
meadow, die Wiese
bud, die Knospe
beech tree, die Buche
veil, der Schleier
smooth, glatt
trunk, der Stamm, ¨e
scent, der Geruch
rustle, rascheln, rauschen

material, der Stoff
lyric poet, der Lyriker
poetry, die Dichtkunst
concern, angehen
publisher, der Verleger
detective story, der Kriminal-
roman
at the latest, spätestens
reluctant, widerwillig

35. BEGINNING OF THE HOLIDAYS

be in the way, einem im Wege
sein
taxi, das Taxi
various things, Verschiedenes
see to, attend to, erledigen,
besorgen
factory, die Fabrik
room, space, seat, der Platz
excuse, die Ausrede
selfish, selbstsüchtig
probably, wahrscheinlich
at least, mindestens
right, correct, richtig
platform, der Bahnsteig

porter, der Gepäckträger
compartment, das Abteil
select, aussuchen
reward, belohnen
tip, das Trinkgeld
overdo it, es zu weit treiben
miss, verpassen, versäumen
anxiously, besorgt
barrier, die Sperre
sight, die Sicht
begin to move, sich in Bewegung setzen
carriage, der Wagen
corridor, der Durchgang

36. IN THE FOG

fog, mist, der Nebel
moor, die Heide
gradually, allmählich
suddenly, plötzlich
thick, dick
cloud, die Wolke
headlight, der Scheinwerfer
light up, beleuchten
reduce, vermindern
visibility, die Sicht
switch off, ausschalten
post, der Pfahl, ¨e
stand (lining a route), Spalier
stehen

engine, der Motor, en
stutter, stottern
dumb, stumm
with the aid of, mittels (*with
Gen.*)
electric torch, die Taschen-
lampe
cause, die Ursache
breakdown, die Panne
petrol, das Benzin
unusual, ausserordentlich
stroke of luck, der Glücksfall
possibility, die Möglichkeit
car, das Auto, der Wagen

daylight, das Tageslicht
traffic, der Verkehr
make up one's mind, sich
　entschliessen, o, o
happen, vorkommen, geschehen
sky, der Himmel
clearly, deutlich
visible, sichtbar
notice, bemerken
straight, gerade

dead straight, schnurgerade
be well acquainted with, gut
　bekannt mit . . . sein
district, die Gegend
turn off (down, into), ein-
　biegen(in), o, o
side road, der Nebenweg,
　Seitenweg
direction, die Richtung

37. THE FIRE

fire, der Brand
fire brigade, die Feuerwehr
flame, die Flamme
protect, schützen
neighbouring, benachbart
case, der Fall, "e
sympathy, die Sympathie
crowd, die Menge
provided, vorausgesetzt
rumour, das Gerücht, e
circulate, umlaufen
owner, der Besitzer
exactly, gerade
inconsolable, trostlos
adequate, ausreichend
compensation, die Entschä-
　digung
insurance, die Versicherung
bankrupt, bankrott
business, das Geschäft
shake, schütteln
sad, traurig
Company, (die) Gesellschaft
& Co., & Co.
firm, die Firma, en
hard-working, fleissig
capable, tüchtig
business man, der Geschäfts-
　mann
deserve, verdienen

honour, die Ehre
elect, wählen (zu)
mayor, der Bürgermeister
successor, der Nachfolger
chip of the old block, vom
　gleichen Schlag
unfortunately, leider
admit, gestehen
pleasure-seeking, vergnüg-
　ungssüchtig
good-for-nothing, der Tau-
　genichts
succumb, erliegen, a, e (with
　Dat.)
late, selig
spoil, verwöhnen
slack, schlaff
administration, die Verwalt-
　ung
go to rack and ruin, zugrunde
　gehen
be on its last legs, auf dem
　letzten Loch pfeifen
come at a convenient time,
　gelegen kommen
arouse, erregen
suspicion, der Verdacht
expect, erwarten
fall in, einstürzen
moment, der Augenblick

general, allgemein
astonishment, das Erstaunen
happen, stattfinden, geschehen, vorkommen

on the contrary, im Gegenteil
disappear, verschwinden, a, u
space of time, die Frist
bad luck, das Pech

38. JOAN ASKS FOR HELP

help, die Hilfe
drive, die Auffahrt
front door, die Haustür
ring a bell, klingeln
stranger, der Fremde (Adj. used as Noun)
pay a call, einen Besuch abstatten
make a fuss, Umstände machen
take offence, Anstoss nehmen (an)
mistake, der Fehler
helpful, hilfreich
kind-hearted, gutherzig
apparently, scheinbar
busy, beschäftigt
ready, bereit
activity, die Tätigkeit, die Beschäftigung
be a matter of, sich handeln um
bottle (Verb), einmachen
solve, lösen
crossword puzzle, das Kreuzworträtsel
remember, sich erinnern (with Gen., or an with Acc.)

ladder, die Leiter
pick, pflücken
introduce, vorstellen
meet, kennenlernen
tennis club, der Tennisklub
make friends with, sich befreunden mit
way of life, die Lebensart
unbearable, unerträglich
seem, vorkommen
to be due to, liegen an
contrast, der Gegensatz, ''e
stepmother, die Stiefmutter
value, schätzen
step, treten, i, a, e
veranda, die Veranda
knitting (piece of), (eine) Strickarbeit
stand, endure, aushalten
escape, entfliehen, o, o
reason, der Grund, ''e
discuss, besprechen
plan, der Plan, ''e
sensible, vernünftig
consider, bedenken
situation, die Lage
dismay, die Bestürzung
reproach, der Vorwurf, ''e

39. ON CHRISTMAS EVE

Christmas Eve, der Weihnachtsabend
doubt, zweifeln
get to, reach, erreichen, ankommen in

clearly, offenbar
different, verschieden
unpleasant, unangenehm
inquiry, die Anfrage
main road, die Hauptstrasse

bad, schlimm
unless, es sei denn, dass
celebrate, feiern
annoy, ärgern
beyond all measure, über alle Massen
spend (time), verbringen
inn, das Wirtshaus
be sorry, bereuen
present, gift, das Geschenk
in advance, im voraus
lug, schleppen
case, der Koffer
unpack, auspacken
razor, der Rasierapparat
toothbrush, die Zahnbürste
the rest, das übrige
borrow, borgen
cousin, der Vetter
away, verreist
hand in, aufgeben

set out, sich auf den Weg machen
dazzling, blendend
unrecognizable, unerkennbar
cover, bedecken
landmark, feature, das Merkmal, e
familiar, das Vertraute
gaze around one, sich umschauen
curiosity, die Neugier
track, die Spur, en
eternal, ewig
snowdrift, die Schneewehe
constantly, beständig
turn aside, abweichen
extremely, äusserst
tiring, ermüdend
ditch, der Graben, ⸚
invisible, unsichtbar
stumble, stolpern

40. THE ELM TREE

elm tree, die Ulme
harbour, cherish, hegen
climb (Tr.), erklettern
huge, gewaltig
topmost, oberst, höchst
branch, der Ast, ⸚e
number, quantity, die Anzahl
rook, crow, die Krähe
untidy, unordentlich
build, bauen
nest; (Verb), das Nest, er; (nisten)
roughly, approximately, ungefähr
circular, rund, kreisförmig
triangular, dreieckig
shape, die Form, Gestalt
recognize (by), erkennen (an)
lack of, der Mangel (an)
symmetry, die Symmetrie

thicket, das Dickicht
shoot, der Schössling
ladder, die Leiter
form, bilden
trunk, der Stamm, ⸚e
serious, ernst
attempt, der Versuch, e
conquer, erobern
private, privat, eigen
rope, das Seil
repeat, wiederholen
failure, das Fehlschlagen
succeed, gelingen (Impers.)
fasten, festmachen
obstacle, das Hindernis, sse
overcome, überwinden, a, u
by far, bei weitem
height, die Höhe
enjoy, geniessen, o, o

unusual, ungewöhnlich
view, die Aussicht
descent, der Abstieg
describe, beschreiben
exploit, die Heldentat
supper, das Abendessen

for once, exceptionally, ausnahmsweise
promise, versprechen
crash down, stürzen
hollow, hohl
rotten, morsch

41. THE TRAMP

tramp, der Landstreicher
accept, annehmen
cheese, der Käse
dignity, die Würde
condition, die Bedingung
earn, verdienen
educated, gebildet
worn out, abgenutzt, abgetragen
material, der Stoff
boot, der Stiefel
expect, erwarten
tie, der Schlips
diagonal, schräg
stripe, der Streifen
significance, die Bedeutung
decipher, entziffern
recently, vor kurzem
barber, der Friseur
all in all, im ganzen genommen
strange, sonderbar
honest, rechtschaffen
hard working, fleissig
citizen, der Bürger
regard, betrachten
able-bodied, rüstig
out of work, unemployed, arbeitslos
approval, benevolence, das Wohlwollen
at any rate, wenigstens
for a change, zur Abwechslung
indicate, weisen, ie, ie (auf)

neglect, vernachlässigen
clip, stutzen, beschneiden, i, i
pleasure, das Vergnügen
fetch, holen
necessary, nötig
tool, das Werkzeug
return, zurückkehren
admit, gestehen
completely, völlig
surprise, überraschen
extremely, äusserst
tired, müde
no wonder, kein Wunder
set, (einem) auferlegen
task, die Aufgabe
avoid, ausweichen, i, i (with Dat.)
conscience, das Gewissen
remorse, der Gewissensbiss, e
supper, das Abendbrot
accept, zusagen
gentle, sanft
courtesy, die Höflichkeit
spend the night, übernachten
barn, die Scheune
mixture, die Mischung
curiosity, die Neugierde, Neugier
envy, der Neid
disapproval, die Missbilligung
interrogate, ausfragen, verhören
behave, sich benehmen

42. IN THE CASTLE

castle, das Schloss, ··er
guide, der Führer
recite, hersagen
fact, die Tatsache
historical, historisch
add, hinzufügen
joke, der Witz
spot, die Stelle
pause, innehalten (sep.)
obedient, gehorsam
procession, der Zug
stay behind, zurückbleiben
linger, verweilen
wall, die Mauer, n
notice, bemerken
offend, beleidigen
official, der Beamte, n
duty, die Pflicht
carry out, erfüllen
patience, die Geduld
skill, das Geschick
atmosphere, die Stimmung
unsatisfactory, ungenügend
ruin, die Ruine
the like, dergleichen
delight, entzücken (Tr.)
staircase, das Treppenhaus
fireplace, der Kamin
be left, übrigbleiben
imagine, sich vorstellen

in those days, at that time,
    damals
compare, vergleichen, i, i
sheer, pure, lauter (invar.)
vanity, die Eitelkeit
believe, glauben
change, die Veränderung
outward, external, äusserlich
circumstance, das Verhältnis
    (Usually pl. in this sense)
effect, die Wirkung
mind, der Geist
feeling, das Gefühl
stand guard, Wache stehen
trench, der Schützengraben
crossbow, die Armbrust
rifle, das Gewehr
make no difference, nichts
    ausmachen
scientific, wissenschaftlich
discovery, die Entdeckung
touch, berühren
surface, die Oberfläche
fundamentally, im Grunde
    genommen
birth, die Geburt
grave, das Grab, ··er
eternal, ewig
spirit, der Geist
call, nennen

43. LONDON

strange, sonderbar, merkwür-
    dig
different, anders
various, verschieden
place, der Ort
alter (Intr.), sich verändern
in the least, im geringsten

building, das Gebäude
absence, die Abwesenheit
disappointment, die Enttäu-
    schung
lie in wait, lauern
visit, besuchen
scene, der Schauplatz

be missing, fehlen
magic, der Zauber
revive, wiederbeleben
depend on, abhängen von
mood, die Stimmung
effect, die Wirkung
consider, halten (für)
capital, die Hauptstadt
centre, die Mitte, das Zentrum
noisy, lärmend, geräuschvoll
superficial, oberflächlich
heartless, herzlos
crazy, verrückt
anthill, der Ameisenhaufen

television aerial, die Fernsehantenne
feeling, das Gefühl
expression, der Ausdruck
disgust, der Widerwille
traveller, der Reisende
compartment, das Abteil
swallow, verschlucken
unpleasant, unangenehm
accent, die Aussprache
regret, bereuen
total (Adj.) gesamt
population, die Bevölkerung
cultured, gebildet

44. THE VISIT

infinitely, unendlich
kind, liebenswürdig
besides, obendrein, ausserdem
distant, entfernt
relative, die Verwandte (Adj. as Noun)
Duchess, die Herzogin
harness, das Geschirr
jingle, klirren
respectful, ehrfurchtsvoll
advantageous, vorteilhaft
coat of arms, das Wappen
ambitious, ehrgeizig, Ehrgeiz haben
society, die Gesellschaft
dazzle, blenden
present, gegenwärtig
circumstance, der Umstand, ⸚e

arouse, erwecken
speculation, Zukunftsträume
curtsey, einen Knicks machen
sunshade, der Sonnenschirm
now and again, ab und zu
avenue, die Allee
spectacle, der Anblick, das Schauspiel
wonder, die Bewunderung
façade, die Fassade
fashion, style, der Stil
pillar, die Säule
right angle, der rechte Winkel
suit, passen (with Dat. or in with Acc.)
nervousness, die Ängstlichkeit
announce, melden

45. THE DOCKS

docks, das Dock is used chiefly in compounds such as "drydock." Use das Hafengebiet
cross, fahren über
Channel, der Kanal
seaside resort, das Seebad

passenger ship, das Passagierschiff
pleasure, das Vergnügen
convenience, die Bequemlichkeit
passenger, der Fahrgast, ⸚e

arrange, einrichten
port, der Hafen
in shirt sleeves, in Hemdärmeln
sight, der Anblick
bring home to, deutlich machen (*with Dat.*)
island, die Insel
vast, ungeheuer
quantity, die Menge
raw material, der Rohstoff
import, einführen
starve, verhungern
hopeless, hoffnungslos
undertaking, das Unterfangen
particular, certain, bestimmt
ship's captain, der Schiffskapitän
turmoil, das Getümmel
difficult, schwierig
after all, schliesslich, letzten Endes
number, die Nummer
wharf, der Kai, s
gangway, das Fallreep

deck, das Deck
doubtful, zweifelhaft
wire rope, das Drahtseil, e
top, die Spitze
crane, der Kran, ¨e
dangle, baumeln
huge, mächtig
bale, der Ballen, –,
gape, klaffen
hold, der Laderaum, ¨e
hoist, heben, o, o
rattle, das Gerassel
machine, die Maschine
sound, der Laut
incomprehensible, unverständlich
order, der Befehl, e
cabin, die Kabine
busy, beschäftigt
heap, der Haufen
tidy up, in Ordnung bringen
look up, aufsehen
rise, sich erheben
offer (hand), reichen

46. THE MISSED TRAIN

miss, versäumen, verpassen
pretty, fairly, ziemlich
short, knapp
terminus, die Endstation
late (of a train), Verspätung haben
connection (train), der Anschlusszug
reach down, herunterholen
case, der Koffer
mackintosh, der Regenmantel
(luggage) rack, das Gepäcknetz
door handle, die Klinke

platform, der Bahnsteig
race, rasen
barrier, die Sperre
no use, umsonst
express, der Eilzug
on time, pünktlich
hand in (deposit), aufgeben
left luggage office, die Gepäckaufbewahrung
client, der Kunde, n, n
public, öffentlich
telephone box, die Fernsprechzelle
desire, die Lust

waiting-room, der Wartesaal
spend (time), verbringen
cinema, das Kino
hopeless, aussichtslos, hoffnungslos
worth seeing, sehenswert
importance, die Bedeutung
junction, der Knotenpunkt
stroll, schlendern
ugly, hässlich
prepared, bereit
public house, das Wirtshaus
enter, call at (of hotel, etc.), einkehren (in *with Dat.*)
distance, die Ferne
unmistakable, unverkennbar
sound, der Lärm
fair, der Jahrmarkt
direction, die Richtung
town hall, das Rathaus
square, der Platz
stall, die Bude
roundabout, das Karussell, e
spectator, der Zuschauer
tower above, überragen (*Tr.*)

framework, scaffolding, das Gerüst
scenic railway, die Achterbahn
entertainment, die Unterhaltung
attract, anziehen, o, o
particularly, besonders
absolutely nothing, gar nichts
get rid of, loswerden (*Tr.*)
small change, das Kleingeld
turn away, sich wegwenden, a, a
ridiculous, lächerlich
nonsense, der Blödsinn
fortune teller, die Wahrsagerin
dish up, tell, vorschwatzen (*with Dat.*)
culmination, zenith, der Hohepunkt
valuable, wertvoll
(piece of) business, das Geschäft
derail, entgleisen
lose one's life, ums Leben kommen

47. TWO FRIENDS

park, der Park
encounter. begegnen (*with Dat.*)
take an interest in, sich interessieren für
flower bed, das Blumenbeet, e
hide, verbergen
smile, lächeln
comical, komisch
present, darstellen
complete, vollkommen
contrast, der Gegensatz
appearance, das Aussehen
judge, urteilen

character, der Charakter, das Gemüt, die Beschaffenheit
thin, mager, dünn
pale, bleich
clean-shaven, glattrasiert
cheek-bone, der Backenknochen, das Wangenbein, e
regardless (of), ohne Rücksicht (auf)
suit, der Anzug
unusual, ungewöhnlich
narrow, schmal, eng
trousers, die Hose(n)
stiff, steif

collar, der Kragen
threaten, drohen
chin, das Kinn
turn, drehen
bowler hat, der Melonenhut
yellow, gelb
glove, der Handschuh, e
tight, straff
roll up, zusammenrollen
umbrella, der Regenschirm
use, benutzen
walking-stick, der Spazierstock
sombre, düster
somewhat, etwas
sinister, unheimlich
figure, die Gestalt, or here: die
Erscheinung
companion, der Gefährte, der
Gesell(e)
shine (with), strahlen (vor)

good nature, die Gutmütigkeit
health, die Gesundheit
colourful, bunt
tie, die Krawatte
silk, seiden
handkerchief. das Taschen-
tuch
breast-pocket, die Brusttasche
buttonhole, das Knopfloch
restrained, zurückhaltend
gloomy, trübsinnig
boisterous, lärmend
affable, leutselig
wave about, schwenken
emphasize, betonen
bench, die Bank, "e
straight, gerade, aufrecht
raise, aufheben, o, o
ground, der Boden
comfortable, bequem
stare at, anstarren

48. ALBRECHT DÜRER

birth, die Geburt
bear, gebären, gebar, geboren
contribute, beitragen
religious, religiös
artist, der Künstler
make available, accessible,
zugänglich machen
woodcut, der Holzschnitt
pity, schade
contemporary, der Zeitgenosse
picture, das Bild
portrait, das Bildnis
drawing, die (Hand) Zeichnung
(oil) painting, das (Öl)
Gemälde
portray, darstellen
strength, die Kraft
courage, der Mut
lead, führen

forehead, die Stirn
wrinkle, die Falte
jut out, hervorragen
sunken, eingesunken
cheek, die Wange
watchful, wachsam
expression, der Ausdruck
suffer, leiden, i, i
embitter, verbittern
terror, der Schrecken
etching, der Kupferstich
knight, der Ritter
devil, der Teufel
use, gebrauchen
figure, die Gestalt
symbol, das Symbol, Sinnbild
frequently, oft, häufig
remind, mahnen an

49. SIEGE OF STRALSUND

siege, die Belagerung
mayor, der Bürgermeister
coast, die Küste
Pomerania, Pommern
be in session, eine Sitzung
  abhalten
anxious, besorgt
Corporation, der Rat
town hall, das Rathaus
resist, widerstehen (*with Dat.*)
attack, der Angriff, e
Imperial, kaiserlich
army, das Heer, die Armee
drive, treiben, ie, ie
Denmark, Dänemark
island, die Insel
people, citizens, die Bürger
steadfastness, die Standhaft-
  igkeit
hardened, proven, bewährt
enemy, der Feind, e
defender, der Verteidiger
cannon, das Geschütz
bombard, beschiessen, o, o
wall, die Mauer, n
respite, der Unterlass
weak, schwach
be capable of, imstande sein
repulse, abschlagen
repeat, wiederholen
assault, der Strum, ̈e
delegate, der Bevollmächtigte
  (*Adj. as Noun*)
hold a parley, eine Unter-
  handlung führen
surrender, submission, die
  Übergabe

honour, with honour, die
  Ehre, ehrenvoll
haughty, hochmütig
court, der Hof
Prague, Prag
leave, verlassen
offer, anbieten, o, o
terms, die Bedingungen
angry, zornig
murmur, grumble, murren
follow, folgen (*with Dat.*)
speech, die Rede
Councillor, der Rat, ̈e
rise, aufstehen, sich erheben
Admiral, der Admiral
Baltic, die Ostsee
quote, zitieren
scornful, höhnisch
fleet, die Flotte
jest, der Witz, e
yield, surrender, sich ergeben
join, sich anschliessen (*with
  Dat.*)
cause, side, die Sache
catholic, katholisch
oppressor, der Bedrücker
chain, die Kette
Heaven, der Himmel
gallant, brave, tapfer
Scot, der Schotte, n
land, landen
prevent, verhindern
take heart, sich ein Herz
  fassen
defeat, die Niederlage

50. A YOUNG PRINCE

possible, möglich, eventuell
consequence, die Folge
event, das Ereignis, sse
important, wichtig
single, einzig
end, enden (*Intr.*)
historian, der Historiker
on occasion, gelegentlich
supposition, die Vermutung
battle, die Schlacht
Crown Prince, der Kronprinz
attempt, versuchen, der Versuch
flee (**from**), entfliehen (*with Dat.*)
tyrannical, tyrannisch
treatment, treat, die Behandlung, behandeln
actually, tatsächlich
take place, stattfinden
flee, fliehen
Dutch, holländisch
frontier, die Grenze
sanctuary, der Zufluchtsort
barn, die Scheune
retinue, das Gefolge
spend the night, übernachten
safety, die Sicherheit

intend, vorhaben
colonel, der Oberst, en
officer, der Offizier, e
order, der Befehl
receive, bekommen
flight, die Flucht
slave, der Sklave, n, n
enraged, entrüstet
slay, umbringen
heir to the throne, der Thronfolger
culprit, der Schuldige
arrest, verhaften
fortress, die Festung
Lieutenant, der Leutnant
accomplice, der Mitschuldige
court martial, das Kriegsgericht
moderate, mässig
sentence, das Urteil
reject, verwerfen
pass (**sentence**)(**on**), fällen (gegen)
personally, persönlich
prison, das Gefängnis
scaffold, das Schafott
forgive, vergeben (*with Dat.*)
in a swoon, ohnmächtig

51. ON A SUMMER'S DAY

Edward, Eduard
measles, die Masern (*f. pl.*)
for the time being, vorläufig, zur Zeit
carrier, der Träger
infectious, ansteckend
disease, die Krankheit
glorious, herrlich
contented, zufrieden
idler, der Faulenzer

satisfy, quieten, beruhigen
conscience, das Gewissen
serve, dienen (*with Dat.*)
pillow, das Kopfkissen
recall (**to mind**), ins Gedächtnis zurückrufen
timetable, der Stundenplan
rock (*Intr.*), sich wiegen
tug, ziehen
gently, sanft

rope, das Seil
fasten, anbinden, a, u
root, die Wurzel
bank, das Ufer
dip, tauchen
lazily, lässig
catch, fangen, ä, i, **a**
leaf, das Blatt, ¨er
float, treiben
at the same time, gleichzeitig, dabei
wonder, das Wunder
sail, segeln
branch, der Ast, Äste
willow tree, die Weide
keep, behalten
shape, die Gestalt, Form
change into, sich verwandeln in (*with Acc.*)
teapot, die Teekanne
make demands, Ansprüche stellen (an)

mental, geistig
faculty, die Fähigkeit
be tired of, (etwas) satt haben
raise, heben, o, o
swallow, die Schwalbe
hunt for, auf der Jagd sein (nach)
insect, das Insekt, en
probably, wahrscheinlich
beak, der Schnabel
the rest, das übrige
chance, der Zufall
self-important, wichtigtuerisch
destroyer, der Zerstörer
escort, guard, bewachen
convoy, der Geleitzug
steer, steuern
examine, untersuchen
devour, verschlingen, a, u
gift, die Gabe, das Geschenk

52. IN THE AIR

air, die Luft
runway, die Startbahn
look, schauen
rush, sausen
disappear, verschwinden, a, u
speed, die Geschwindigkeit
automatically, automatisch, unwillkürlich
seek, feel for, tasten nach
parachute, der Fallschirm
serve, dienen
paratrooper, der Fallschirmjäger
aeroplane, das Flugzeug
arrival, die Ankunft
peaceful, friedvoll
by comparison, im Vergleich
experience, erleben

provided, vorausgesetzt
customs official, der Zollbeamte, n
examine, untersuchen
brief-case, die Mappe
concern oneself with, sich kümmern um
chiefly, hauptsächlich
be interested in, sich interessieren für
jewel, das Juwel, en
scent, das Parfüm
stocking, der Strumpf, ¨e
and so on, und so weiter (usw)
calm oneself, sich beruhigen
enjoy, geniessen, o, o
journey, die Reise

comfortable, bequem
upholstered, gepolstert
seat, der Sitz, e; der Stuhl, ¨e
civil (civilian), Zivil-
metal, metallen
bench, die Bank, ¨e
transport plane, das Transportflugzeug
jet engine, der Düsenmotor
in many respects, in vieler Hinsicht
surprising, erstaunlich
difference, der Unterschied
admire, bewundern
cloud, die Wolke
level, eben

surface, die Oberfläche
gleam, leuchten
brilliant, glänzend
cotton wool, die Watte
huge, gewaltig
wing (of plane), die Tragfläche
motionless, bewegungslos
incredible, unglaublich
in fact, in der Tat
destination, das Reiseziel
glimpse, erblicken
now and then, ab und zu
need, gebrauchen
cover (distance), zurücklegen
distance, die Strecke

53. FREDERICK AND VOLTAIRE

architect, der Baumeister
within, innerhalb (*with Gen.*)
generation, das Menschenalter
conquer, erobern
use, gebrauchen, sich bedienen (*with Gen.*)
native tongue, die Muttersprache
address, anreden
poison, das Gift
bundle, das Bündel
verse, der Vers
poem, das Gedicht
note, merken, bemerken
throne, der Thron
attack, der Angriff
author, der Schriftsteller
ape, nachäffen (*sep.*)
classicism, der Klassizismus
publish, veröffentlichen
urgent, dringend
invitation, die Einladung
rebel, der Rebell, en, en

compel, zwingen
flee (from), entfliehen aus
unworthy, unwürdig
malicious pleasure, die Schadenfreude
disappoint, enttäuschen
philosopher, der Philosoph
grasping, geizig
petty, kleinlich
admire, bewundern
despise, verachten
for his part, seinerseits
doubtful, zweifelhaft
correct, verbessern
remark, bemerken
wash, waschen
linen, die Wäsche
rude, unhöflich
wonder, das Wunder
quarrel, sich zanken
unedifying, unerbaulich, unerfreulich

54. GOOD ADVICE

gaze, schauen
silent, schweigend
fade, verbleichen, i, i
general, allgemein
presence, die Gegenwart
pardon, die Entschuldigung
past, die Vergangenheit
switch on, andrehen
curtain, der Vorhang, ˸e; die Gardine
opposite, gegenüber (with Dat.)
unsympathetic, teilnahmslos
advice, der Rat
ask for, bitten, a, e (um)
flattering, schmeichelhaft
after all, am Ende doch
experience, die Erfahrung
pass on, überliefern
fruit, die Frucht, ˸e
mistake, der Fehler
avoid, vermeiden
suffering, das Leid
disappointment, die Enttäuschung
dangerous, gefährlich
assume, annehmen
similar, ähnlich
cause, die Ursache
same, gleich
result, die Folge
produce, hervorbringen
circumstance, das Verhältnis, sse; der Umstand, ˸e

identical, identisch
human being, der Mensch, en, en
choose, wählen
profession, der Beruf
enter, eintreten in
career, die Laufbahn
to all appearances, allem Anschein nach
suit, passen (zu)
ability, die Fähigkeiten
character, der Charakter
win, erringen, a, u
happiness, das Glück
wealth, der Reichtum
on the other hand, andererseits
succeed, gelingen, a, u. (Es ist mir gelungen)
reach, erreichen
favourable, günstig
opportunity, die Gelegenheit
cross-roads, der Scheideweg
dull, langweilig
security, die Sicherheit
charm, der Reiz
unknown, unbekannt
reluctant, abgeneigt
express, äussern
opinion, die Meinung
regret, bereuen
decision, die Entscheidung (treffen)

55. THE COLLISION

midnight, die Mitternacht
accident, das Unglück
dream, der Traum, ˸e
all manner of, allerlei
event, das Ereignis, sse

take place, vorkommen, stattfinden
last, dauern
occupy, ausfüllen
reality, die Wirklichkeit

fraction, der Bruchteil
second, die Sekunde
rock, wanken
shock, der Stoss, ¨e
earthquake, das Erdbeben
crack, die Spalte, der Riss, e
everywhere, überall
tile, der Ziegel
notice, bemerken
yell, brüllen
collapse, zusammenstürzen
stare, starren
porthole, das Bullauge
reflection, der Widerschein
fog, der Nebel
outside, draussen
recoil, zurückfahren
mutual, gegenseitig
astonishment, das Erstaunen
gaze, schauen
lighted, erleuchtet
cabin, die Kajüte
Atlantic, der Atlantik
tremendous, gewaltig
din, das Getöse
drown (of noise), übertönen
regular, regelmässig

interval, der Abstand, ¨e
deep (of sound), dumpf
moan, stöhnen
fog-horn, das Nebelhorn
sailor, der Matrose, n
hurry, eilen
bows, der Bug
searchlight, der Scheinwerfer
light up, illuminate, beleuchten
figure, die Gestalt
work with, handle, hantieren mit
rope, das Tau, e
plank, das Brett, er
explain, erklären
attach oneself, sich anschliessen (*with Dat.*)
appear, auftauchen
collision, der Zusammenstoss
inevitable, unavoidable, unvermeidlich
thanks to, dank (*with Dat.*)
helmsman, der Steuermann
damage, der Schaden
gape open, klaffen

56. "OLD FRITZ"

campaign, der Feldzug
exact, genau
spend (time), verleben
rule, regieren
accession, die Thronbesteigung
unimportant, unbedeutend
kingdom, das Königreich
rank, der Rang
power, die Macht, ¨e
effect, erzielen
change, die Änderung
sacrifice, aufopfern
forbear, der Vorfahr, en

amass, ansammeln
Silesia, Schlesien
hold, keep, behalten
utterly, vollkommen
devastate, verwüsten
impoverish, verarmen
ruthless, rücksichtslos
efficiency, die Gründlichkeit
characterize, kennzeichnen
conduct, die Führung
genius, das Genie
remarkable, merkwürdig
busy itself, sich beschäftigen

task, die Aufgabe
peaceful, friedvoll
reconstruction, der Wiederaufbau
foster, fördern
development, die Entwicklung
industry, die Industrie
trade, der Handel
forbid, verbieten, o, o
import, die Einfuhr
cotton, die Baumwolle, Baumwoll —
silk, die Seide, Seiden —
linen, das Leinen, Leinen —
wool, woollen, die Wolle, wollen
goods, die Waren
send, schicken
expert, der Fachmann
study, studieren
tool, das Werkzeug
method, die Methode

administration, die Verwaltung
state, der Staat
field (fig.), das Gebiet
personal, persönlich
supervision, die Aufsicht
servant, der Diener
transform, verwandeln
stiff, steif
stern, streng
figure, die Gestalt
benevolent, wohlwollend
despot, der Despot
society, die Gesellschaft
body, der Körper
act, handeln
community, die Gemeinschaft
powerful, mächtig
machine, die Maschine
sense (meaning), die Bedeutung

57. THE FLOOD

the unknown, das Unbekannte
drive mad, zum Wahnsinn treiben
experience, erleben
danger, die Gefahr
obvious, offenbar, klar
pray, beten
continuous, ununterbrochen, beständig
coward, der Feigling
literally, buchstäblich
joke, der Spass
dam, die Talsperre
sweep, fegen, stürzen
drown, ertrinken, a, u (Intr.); ertränken (weak. Tr.)
flood, die Überschwemmung

escape, entkommen (with Dat.)
be aware of, etwas gewahr werden
rush, sausen
rumble, poltern, brausen
tremble, zittern
landing, der Flur
in a twinkling, im Nu
bump, stossen
ceiling, die Decke
go out (of light), erlöschen, o, o
Flood, die Sintflut
dry, trocken
darkness, die Finsternis, die Dunkelheit
dawn, der Sonnenaufgang
fearful, schrecklich, furchtbar

58. IN THE MUNICIPAL THEATRE

municipal theatre, das Stadttheater

seat, der (Sitz) platz, ``e

taken, occupied, besetzt

audience, das Publikum, die Zuschauer (*pl.*)

prepared, bereit

overlook, übersehen (*insep.*)

shortcoming, die Unzulänglichkeit

presentation, performance, die Aufführung

act, spielen

girls' grammar school, das Lyzeum

boys' grammar school, das Gymnasium

assembly hall, die Aula

destroy, zerstören

air-raid, der Luftangriff, e

possess, besitzen, a, e

hall, der Saal, Säle

to be suitable, geeignet für

occasion, event, die Veranstaltung

jointly, gemeinsam

rent, mieten

certain, gewiss

opposition, der Widerstand

plan, der Plan, ``e

carry out, durchführen

speech, die Rede, Ansprache

prize-giving, die Preisverteilung

clap, klatschen

sore, wund

offend, beleidigen

neighbour, der Nachbar, s, n, n

accord, spenden

applause, der Beifall

strive, sich anstrengen

conceal, verbergen, i, a, o

boredom, die Langeweile

glad, froh

interval, die Pause

stage, die Bühne

clear, räumen

arrange, einrichten

comedy, das Lustspiel, e

extract, der Auszug, ``e

Lover's Caprice, die Laune des Verliebten

light-hearted, heiter

sentimental, sentimental

charming, anmutig, reizend

delightful, entzückend

opportunity, die Gelegenheit

stamp, aufstampfen

shout, schreien, ie, ie

push, stossen, ie, o

perform, vorführen, aufführen, spielen

bourgeois General, der Bürgergeneral

finally, schliesslich, zum Schluss

scene, die Szene, der Auftritt

memory, die Erinnerung

poet, der Dichter

appear, erscheinen, ie, ie

original, Ur-

version, die Fassung

play, das Schauspiel

disguised, verkleidet

exploit, ausnützen

fame, der Ruhm

reputation, der Ruf

learned, gelehrt

doctor, der Doktor, s, en

bewilder, verwirren

corrupt, verführen

inexperienced, unerfahren

freshman, der Fuchs

59. THE GREAT ELECTOR

Elector, der Kurfürst
fortunate, ein Glück
fate, das Schicksal
Prussia, Preussen
exceptional, ausserordentlich
gifted, begabt
ironic, ironisch
chance, der Zufall
vain, eitel
extravagant, verschwenderisch
exchange (for), vertauschen (mit)
claim (to), der Anspruch (auf)
fame, der Ruhm
great-grandfather, der Urgrossvater
be successful, erfolgreich sein, Erfolg haben
restoration, die Wiederherstellung, der Wiederaufbau
will-power, die Willenskraft
energy, die Energie
regard, betrachten
founder, creator, der Gründer, Stifter
spirit, der Geist
measure, die Massregel, Massnahme
benevolent, wohltätig

useful, nützlich, von Nutzen
arise from, entstehen aus
desire, wish, der Wunsch
persecute, verfolgen
religious, religiös
on . . . grounds, aus . . . Gründen
stern, streng
ambassador, der Gesandte
order, der Befehl
invite, einladen, auffordern
emigrate, auswandern
settle, sich niederlassen
service, der Gottesdienst
hold (service), abhalten
community, die Gemeinde
cradle, die Wiege
colony, die Kolonie
consist of, bestehen aus
revocation, die Aufhebung
edict, das Edikt
announce, bekanntgeben
refuge, der Zufluchtsort
policy, die Politik
citizen, der Bürger
exercise influence, Einfluss ausüben
favourable, günstig
development, die Entwicklung

60. THE LOVER OF ANIMALS

lover of animals, der Tierfreund
acquaintance, die Bekanntschaft
adventurous, abenteuerlich
be interested in, sich interessieren für
protect, beschützen

squirrel, das Eichhörnchen
tame, zahm
magpie, die Elster
hawk, der Habicht, der Falke
toad, die Kröte
adder, die Natter
object, Einwände machen
be grown up, erwachsen sein

veterinary surgeon, der Tierarzt
knowledge, die Kenntnis, se
animals, animal kingdom, die Tierwelt
famous, berühmt
collect, catch, sammeln, fangen, ä, i, a
collection, die Sammlung
all kinds of, allerlei (*invar.*)
zoo, der Tiergarten, der Zoo, s
stuff, ausstopfen

exhibit, zur Schau stellen
souvenir, das Andenken
various, verschieden
modest, bescheiden
boast, prahlen
suffer, leiden
captivity, die Gefangenschaft
circus, der Zirkus
ill-treat, misshandeln
on the contrary, im Gegenteil
trick, das Kunststück